WINTER TRAILS

winter ™
trails

MICHIGAN

The Best Cross-Country Ski
& Snowshoe Trails

by
WILLIAM SEMION

The
Globe
Pequot
Press

GUILFORD, CONNECTICUT

Winter Trails is a trademark of The Globe Pequot Press.

Cover photographs: top, courtesy Redfeather; bottom, courtesy Tubbs Snowshoe Co., Stowe, Vermont
Cover and interior design: Nancy Freeborn
Trail maps created by Equator Graphics © The Globe Pequot Press
Photo credits: page 1: Bill Semion photo; page 6: ©Terry W. Phipps/courtesy Mackinac Island Chamber of Commerce; page 9: Dixie Franklin photo; page 18: © 1998 AAA Michigan/Robert Brodbeck; page 26: Rah Trost photo; page 31: Bill Semion photo; page 36: Frida Waara photo; page 39: Dixie Franklin photo; page 43: courtesy Porcupine Mountains State Park; page 50: courtesy Active Backwoods Retreats; page 55: courtesy Kalamazoo Nature Center; page 59: courtesy Yankee Springs Recreation Area; page 63: courtesy Ottawa County Parks & Recreation Commission; page 67: courtesy Muskegon County Convention and Visitors Bureau; page 76: courtesy Cool's Cross-Country Farm Trails; page 86: courtesy Crystal Mountain Resort; page 102: courtesy Village Press, Inc.; page 110: courtesy Boyne USA Resorts; page 125: HCMA photo; page 133: HC Metroparks photo; page 140: courtesy For-Mar Nature Preserve and Arboretum; page 144: courtesy Gary Nelkie; page 149: Bill Semion photo; page 153: Bill Semion photo; page 157: photo courtesy Forbush Corner; page 161: courtesy Treetops Sylvan Resort; page 168: courtesy Wilderness Valley; page 172: Bill Semion photo; page 176: courtesy Thunder Bay Resort

Library of Congress Cataloging-in-Publication Data

Semion, William.
    Winter trails Michigan : the best cross-country ski & snowshoe trails / by William Semion.— 1st ed.
        p. cm. — (Winter trails series)
    ISBN 0-7627-0304-0
    1. Skis and skiing—Michigan—Guidebooks. 2. Snowshoes and snowshoeing—Michigan—Guidebooks. 3. Cross-country ski trails—Michigan—Guidebooks. 4. Michigan—Guidebooks. I. Title. II. Series.

GV854.5.M5 S46 2000
917.7404'4—dc21   00-032142

Manufactured in the United States of America
First Edition/First Printing

Contents

Michigan

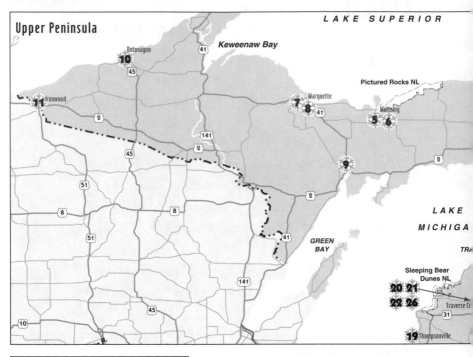

Upper Peninsula

LAKE SUPERIOR

Keweenaw Bay

Ontonagon
10
45
41

Ironwood
11
2

Pictured Rocks NL

Marquette
7 8
41
Munising
5 6

141
2

45
2
9
2

51
8
8
2
141

51
GREEN
BAY
LAKE
MICHIGA

TR

Sleeping Bear
Dunes NL
20 21
22 26
Traverse Ci
31

141
45
10

19 Thompsonville

MICHIGAN AND SURROUNDING AREA

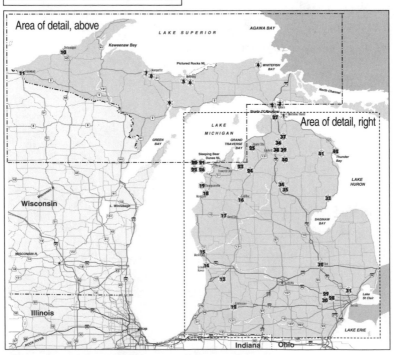

Area of detail, above

LAKE SUPERIOR
AGAWA BAY
Keweenaw Bay
10
Pictured Rocks NL
WHITEFISH
BAY
7 8
Munising
5 6
North Channel

LAKE
MICHIGAN
GRAND
TRAVERSE
BAY
27
Area of detail, right
25
37
36
38 39
35
41
42
Thunder
Bay
Sleeping Bear
Dunes NL
20 21
22 26
23
24
34
35
33
19 Thompsonville
LAKE
HURON
GREEN
BAY
16
SAGINAW
BAY
Wisconsin
L. Winnebago
17
WISCONSIN R.
15
14
13
30
32
29 31
30
Lake
St Clair
Illinois
12
LAKE ERIE
Indiana   Ohio

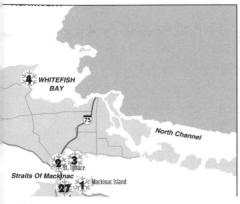

Note: Numbers on map correspond with trails numbered in the table of contents.

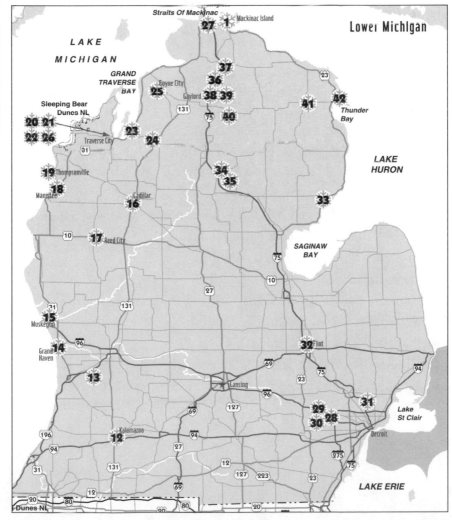

Preface

The silent sound of skis slipping through the snow. The wail of the wind whistling though the pines, roaring, then stilled as you enter farther into the protection of the heart of a forest, before bursting into a sun so bright even shades don't help as you slide down a hill where young pines sprout all around your boots.

Those sounds of skis biting across an exposed root or newly fallen twig. That little tickly zzzzzip vibrating into your boots to the sole, and the realization that, somehow, it and you have been put at that spot at that same moment in time that perhaps will never come again. The views as you stand at an overlook and see nothing but treetops for miles.

Try explaining it all to someone who is not an outdoors lover, and sorry, but they just don't get it.

All those experiences and more are part of a ski adventure in Michigan. If you're a skier, you know what I mean. And if you're still a bit wobbly on your skis and think that a beginner run is just fine for now, thank you, you will learn soon enough.

Michigan doesn't have the mountains of Colorado or Montana. Thank goodness. I do so miss all that gasping for breath and those lactated muscles I experience whenever I strap on a pair of skinny skis in the mountains. Miss 'em like a ninety-degree turn at the bottom of a screamer of a hill. What we lack in the mountains' spectacular beauty, we make up for with a different kind. Beauty in things both large and small that every skier can relate to. In whatever degree that suits them, skiers in Michigan have the unique opportunity to experience that same oneness with nature, whether out on a crisp day in February, or on an early March afternoon when the sun is already transforming the snow into those clear ice crystals that foretell the coming of spring.

There are more than 3,400 kilometers of trails in the state to explore. We Michigan skiers are lucky, too because we can experience all that beauty on trails that are in every corner of the state, from those only a short drive from the state's major cities, or a lonely trail deep in an Upper Peninsula forest, where wolf tracks might mingle with your own. Each year Michigan skiers experience all that. And now, it's waiting for you, too.

In this book, I've tried to give you a taste of what's available, from trails near the city, to some of the most remote in the state, from the most famous, to the most humble. There are plenty more where these came from too, ones that, due to space and time, I had to leave out. But what are included are favorites of mine and lots of others. You'll find 'em on both state and national forest land, and even on private property. They're all here to be enjoyed and they all should be.

Don't be afraid to tackle any of them regardless of whether you think they're too close or too remote, because each lends its own experience and history to yours. Hopefully in a season or two, you can visit those listed here, and others, and you can discover your favorites.

So lace- or buckle-into those skis and snowshoes, and wherever you go to enjoy the season, prepare to be dazzled by the brilliance of Michigan's winters outdoors. See you on the trail!

A Word about the Maps

U.S. Geological Survey maps—topographic maps—form the underlying basis of the trail maps in this book. The U.S. Geological Survey is in the process of converting its topographic maps from feet to meters. Because this is an ongoing project, not every U.S. Geological Survey map has been converted. Therefore, you will find that on some maps in this book, elevations appear in feet while on others they appear in meters. A box on the map tells you if the elevations are in meters.

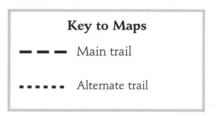

Key to Icons	Key to Maps
▬ cross-country skiing trail	▬ ▬ ▬ Main trail
▰ snowshoeing trail	
◄ skate skiing (skating) trail	▪▪▪▪▪▪ Alternate trail

Note: Miles and kilometers are both used in this book to indicate distances. One kilometer equals .62 mile.

Acknowledgments

A book such as this is most often a team effort, and it's time to acknowledge some of the unsung members of that team, including all those who helped in the research, from Scott Renas on the telephone, to folks like Ron Welton at Porcupine Mountains State Park and Chip Francke at tiny Pigeon Creek Park, to Laura Bollman, whose loving understanding of the time and effort such a project takes, and to my daughter Sonya, whose proofing helps ensure that when you dial a phone number, it will connect, and to my son Justin, who skied with me to provide some of the memories herein. And to all those others who helped me in this effort but go unnamed, but know who they are, thank you. Without you it wouldn't have been possible to share these trails with others.

michigan

Upper Peninsula

This is where cross-country really gets serious. Large glacial, often rocky hills. Big, consistent snowfalls and temperatures that hold the white stuff on the ground well into early April. Deep hardwood and conifer forests that look like they haven't been disturbed in eons. Huge expanses of land, long trails, and, except for the weekends, few, if any other people on a lot of the systems, all spread across an area that reaches nearly the breadth of the Midwest. You'll see some trails on gentle dunes near major cities, and others in hidden spots in some of the wildest sections of Middle America.

If you're interested in more skiing, some of the best sources of information include the Hiawatha and Ottawa National Forests, local State Department of Natural Resources offices, as well as local convention and visitors bureaus, most of which have free maps, or at least information, on their respective areas. Here's a glimpse at just a few of the many trails that await your skis.

Mackinac Island State Park Trails
Mackinac Island State Park, Mackinac Island

Trail type:	▬▬ ⬭
Location:	On the eastern side of Mackinac Island, between the Lower and Upper Peninsulas.
Also used by:	No one. This part of the island is closed to snowmobiling.
Distance:	6 miles of trails over 14 loops.
Terrain:	Some of the most beautiful in the state, with incomparable views of the Upper and Lower Peninsulas and the Mackinac Bridge. Most trails are rolling, with hills no more than 30 to 40 feet high. The exception is one spot coming down off Fort Holmes, the island's highest point, where British forces forced the surrender of the American-held Fort Mackinac during the War of 1812; there, it's a 100 foot drop with a sharp left-hander that's hard to handle for all but the best skiers.
Trail difficulty:	More difficult, except for one run down from the top of the island at Fort Holmes, which is rated most difficult.
Surface quality:	Groomed as needed. Mostly single track set, with a few areas of double track.
Food and facilities:	While the storied Grand Hotel closes in late October, several others stay open year-round, including Mission Point Resort, with 129 rooms and suites, a movie theater, and hot tubs. There are also condos, several downtown restaurants, and a general store. Ski rentals are available at the Village Inn Restaurant. There are no other trail or use fees. Skiers are requested to sign in at the trailhead at the tip of South Bicycle Trail near Fort Mackinac. There's one pine box at the trailhead and another at the corner of Crooked Tree and Garrison Roads. Trail maps provided by the island chamber of commerce are very hard to read. Study them using the island's summertime trail map too. Still, you needn't worry about getting lost. It's an island, remember? There are lots of signs. There's a medical center on the island and a hospital in Cheboygan.
	Ferry service to the island ends January 2. Thereafter, boats run as weather permits. Call Arnold Transit for times. Flights to the island from St. Ignace cost about $15 each way. Or you can tempt the fates and travel by snowmobile across the ice from St. Ignace on the Upper Peninsula side of the Mackinac Bridge. This can be done only in the dead of winter, and if you're not going with a local, it is definitely not recommended.

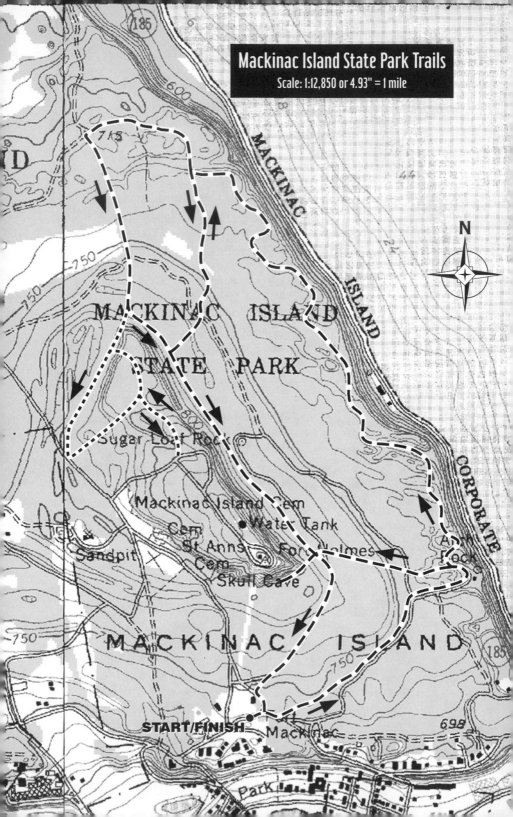

Mackinac Island State Park Trails
Scale: 1:12,850 or 4.93" = 1 mile

185

600

750

750

713

MACKINAC ISLAND

STATE PARK

MACKINAC ISLAND

Sugar Loaf Rock

Mackinac Island Cem

Cem
St Anns
Cem
Skull Cave

Water Tank

Fort Holmes

Sandpit

Arch
Rock

CORPORATE

MACKINAC ISLAND

750

750

185

698

START/FINISH

Mackinac

Park

N

Phone numbers: Mission Point Resort reservations, (800) 833–7711. Arnold Transit, (906) 643–7327. Air transport from St. Ignace, (906) 643–7165. Village Inn Restaurant, (906) 847–3591. Contact the chamber of commerce at (800) 4–LILACS for information; Web sites, www.mackinacisland.org or www.mackinac.com.

WANT TO EXPERIENCE Mackinac Island as close as you can to the way it was in the 18th and 19th centuries with the added luxuries that you'll experience back at your hotel or B&B room? Come here in winter. There may be no more serene and beautiful spots in the state than what you'll find on the trails of the island. Locals will tell that this is how the island is meant to be seen, devoid of summer's crowds and filled with quiet. You can glide by some of the finest examples of Victorian-era "cottages" found anywhere. Trails are well kept but little used, except by a handful of locals who ski regularly. The entire northern side of the island is blocked off and available to skiers and snowshoers only.

The most popular routes start out almost from the base of the walls of Fort Mackinac, occupied by British and Americans starting more than 200 years ago. No cars are allowed on the island. All transportation in summer is by either horse or bicycle. All the trails you'll be on are rated more difficult, and most are bike paths groomed for skiing.

Start out by climbing the overlook from downtown along Fort Street past the Michigan governor's residence, then up to the fort until you're at the start of South Bicycle Trail. It's a good idea to take off your skis on the climb up, because it's a pretty good one. Start off on a straight shot along South Bicycle Trail, a nice, flat route that runs for a good 0.25 mile. You'll then encounter the only sign on the trail, warning you—bicyclists actually—of the impending 45-foot gradual drop that will turn to your left a bit before ending at one of the island's favorite overlooks, Arch Rock. It's probably the steepest part of your entire journey. This is a natural limestone formation high on a bluff that looks out to the edge of the land

Directions at a glance

MILE

0.0 From behind Fort Mackinac head out on South Bicycle Trail.

0.5 Turn left at Arch Rock onto Leslie Avenue.

1.5 Turn left onto Murray Trail.

1.75 Turn left onto Crooked Tree Road.

2.2 Turn left onto Juniper Trail.

2.3 Join with North Bicycle Trail.

3.0 Turn left onto Garrison Road.

3.1 Return to start.

A scenic view at Mackinac Island State Park.

and into Lake Huron. It's a beautiful sight at any time of year. Take off your skis and climb onto the platform for a good look.

From here you can decide what you want to do. If you want to head back to town, there are a couple of ways to go. The first trail to your left from Arch Rock is Huron Road. It's a beautifully rolling trail with one moderate 30-foot drop that will lead you past Robinson's Folly, of which several local tales describe how it got its name. You'll come out of the trees above Mission Point Resort into what most who've seen it on a sunny day describe as one of the most beautiful views in America, with the Mackinac Bridge in the background and Michigan's Lower Peninsula framed by the snow-covered ice of the Mackinac Straits.

Continue on past the great summer homes along this wonderful bluff back to the fort and then back down Fort Street and you'll have gone about 3 miles. You can also extend your trek by going up South Bicycle Trail, north on North Bicycle Trail, and back again via Rifle Range Trail to the fort.

More intrepid skiers who want to see a bit more of the island can continue from Arch Rock northward into the woods along Leslie Avenue. It follows right along the high bluff on the northeastern side of the island, squiggling along with overlooks of the lakeshore.

This section is usually double tracked with no obstacles. There are a couple of ways to return here on trails that intersect with Leslie. Head back on Murray Trail, Soldier's Garden, or Scott's Trail, which you'll meet in that order. All lead left from Leslie and are gradual climbs up to Crooked Tree Road. You can actually extend this part of the trip by first taking Murray Trail to Crooked Tree, turning right, and going north again onto Soldier's, then turning left and taking Leslie to Scott's Trail, where you'll again turn left for the climb back to Crooked Tree. From there head on Juniper Trail back to North Bicycle Trail, which takes you back to the start near the fort. Do that and you've probably gone a good 10 kilometers.

To get to the island's highest point, Fort Holmes, take Cliff View and Beechwood to one of the prettiest-named trails on the island, Morning Snack. It leads to a portion of Fort Holmes Road. There are two lookouts, one called Lookout Point along Fort Holmes, the highest point on the island. Getting down, you'll have to handle that hard run on Henry Trail. Where the route takes a serious left turn in the middle, at the bottom of a 100-foot drop, you'll find more sitzmarks than anywhere else, because the turn psychs out most skiers in a hurry. From there it's a short trip via Rifle Range Trail back to the fort.

Snowshoers can avail themselves of any of the trails as long as they stay off the set tracks. Or head off on your own adventure down any of the other wonderfully named little routes into the woods, including Coffee, Burl, Lost Bear, and Tranquil Bluff. You won't get lost if you've got a map, or even if you don't. The island is perfect for exploring during this quiet time of year.

Sand Dunes Ski Trail

Hiawatha National Forest, St. Ignace

Trail type: ▬▬▬

Note: all one-way except for one section of Loop A.

Location: In the Hiawatha National Forest, approximately 18 miles west of St. Ignace off U.S. 2. Take Brevort Lake Road north about 0.5 mile to the trailhead parking lot on your left.

Also used by: No one.

Distance: 7.6 miles on seven trails.

Terrain: You'll be heading over and up and down former Lake Michigan sand dunes that are for the most part heavily wooded, with some bare, windblown areas as well. Elevations change about 108 feet, from nearly level with the lake at the parking area, to the highest hills at 100 feet elevation, especially on Loops F and G.

Trail difficulty: Easiest to most difficult.

Surface quality: Groomed once a week.

Food and facilities: Food is available in St. Ignace about 11 miles east, or in Brevort 10 miles west, both along U.S. 2. Accommodations nearby include St. Ignace's Comfort Inn, with 100 rooms, an indoor pool, and an exercise area. Also, Brevort's Clearwater Resort Hotel has 19 condo-style rooms, a restaurant, and racquetball courts. You'll find pit toilets and a log-cabin warming hut with woodstove at the trailhead. It's up to you to build a fire. No water. Rentals and tuning are available at St. Ignace. There's a hospital in St. Ignace.

Phone numbers: St. Ignace ranger office, (906) 643–7900. St. Ignace Comfort Inn, (906) 643–7733. Clearwater Resort Hotel & Condos, (906) 292–5506. St. Ignace Tourist Association, (906) 643–6950 or (800) 338–6660; Web site, www.visit-usa.com. mackinac.

THE LAKE MICHIGAN shoreline between St. Ignace and Brevort is one of the state's most beautiful in any season. In summer cars line U.S. 2's shoulder as soon as the dunes that buffer the shoreline here become visible. Families clamor out to enjoy the lake along the highway, which winds close to the water for a good 10 miles. In winter a few head for this trail system, in the same general area. The trailhead is at the site of Round Lake CCC Camp, which located here in 1935. Civilian Conservation Corps members were responsible for planting many of the pines you'll see here to help stabilize the shifting sands and start building soil. It's a wonderfully secluded ski area that doesn't see much traffic.

Loop A is on gentle terrain right next to the steep dunes, so it's perfect for beginners and as a warm-up, cool-down run for accomplished skiers. It begins by taking a right from the parking area and snaking through the low dunes with few hills and no sharp turns. While you're on the trail, be sure to glance at the gray bark of the beech trees along the way, especially in the area named Bearclaw—with good reason. You'll see vertical streaks on the trees in several locations. They're black bear claw marks, left as the animals climb the trees looking for beechnuts in the fall. The bears are not around in winter.

Loop A meets 1.5-mile-long Loop B at Hemlock Hollow, so named for the trees in this low section. This section of the trail is two-way, because it's also part of Loop B. Loop A heads down through the Bearclaw area and then turns left for a 0.7-mile glide back to the lot. Loop B allows both beginners and intermediate skiers to go together. The more enthusiastic in your party can tackle 100-foot-high hills like Ridge Runner, Omigosh, and Wildcat, a particularly interesting one with a wicked right turn at the bottom, while beginners can take two routes that bypass all those hills. Loop B also passes two ponds near its start, a larger one on your right and a smaller on the left side of the route. On

Sand Dunes Trail is a secluded trek over tree-covered dunes pushed up by Lake Michigan winds.

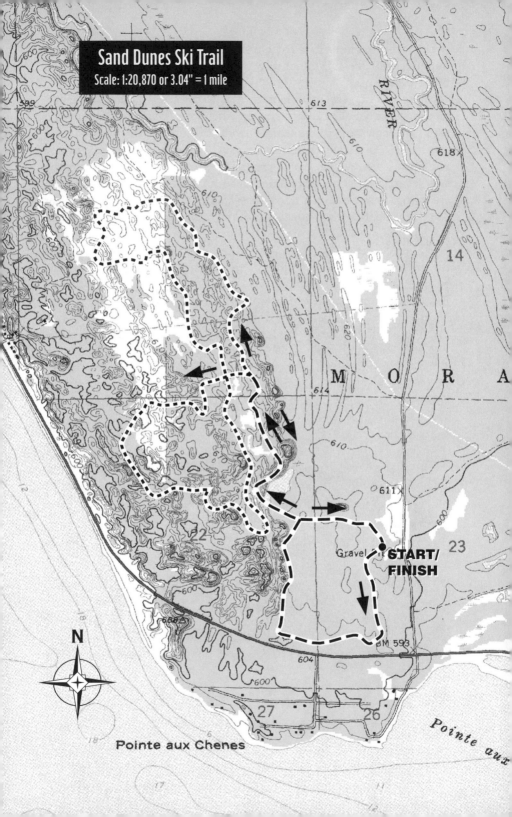

Loop B and C you'll pass through plantations of short conifers, jack pines planted by CCC workers in 1935. Mixed in are natural oaks and white pines.

Pick up the 1.8-mile Loop C at the intersection where Loop B is its farthest north and makes its left turn after Wildcat Hill before turning again for home. C's rated more difficult, and Get Down, the first drop, is one reason why. This curving right-hander falls 100 feet before making a hairpin left that has "Watch Out!" written all over it. The track then makes another bump or two before meeting with D, a 0.8-mile intermediate area that's in a wide-open part of the dunes. This one may be tricky or even unskiable despite the fact that all the other trails have plenty of snow on them, because of its susceptibility to winds off the lake. If it doesn't look to be in good shape, continue on C and reenter the protection of the pines.

Directions at a glance

MILE

MILE	
0.0	Go right from parking lot onto Loop A.
0.3	Turn left at first intersection.
0.6	Turn left at intersection.
1.9	Return to start

If you tackle Loop E, a very challenging more-difficult run because of hills up to 75 feet in elevation, along with runs at the bottom of spots like Sandslide and Silicon Valley—another reference to the dunes—that'll make your ski tips curl, look for the Eolian Hills, some of the largest dunes in the area at upward of 75 feet. Loops F and G, at about 3 and 1.5 miles respectively, should be left for advanced skiers, because there are some hefty hills with steep turns in the middle and at the ends of each.

Sand Dunes is a great little area that doesn't get skied much, but it's definitely deserving of your attention.

McNearney Trail
Hiawatha National Forest, Strongs Corner

Trail type: ▬ ◄ ▩

Note: All ski trails are one-way. A short skating loop is the beginner's loop. Snowshoeing is off piste.

Location: In the eastern Hiawatha National Forest, 5 miles northeast of Strongs Corner and 25 miles east of Brimley. From Brimley follow MI 28 to Strongs. Turn north onto FR 3159 (Salt Point Road) for 5 miles. The trailhead is on the western side of the road at the end of a sweeping right-hand curve.

Also used by: No one. No motorized vehicles are allowed on the trail.

Distance: 9 miles in four loops from 1 to 3 miles long.

Terrain: Heavily wooded trails in the Hiawatha National Forest, covered with second-growth hardwoods and pines. Elevation change is mostly moderate, with a maximum on one trail of 75 feet. The hills at the end of one loop, however, should be approached by advanced skiers only.

Trail difficulty: Easiest to most difficult.

Surface quality: Groomed and single track set regularly, averaging once a week.

Food and facilities: There's a log cabin with woodstove and pit toilet at the trailhead. No water. Restaurants are found in Sault Ste. Marie and Brimley. Accommodations in Sault Ste. Marie (nicknamed The Soo) include the restored 1928 Ojibway Hotel downtown, with 71 rooms, an indoor pool, and an exercise room. Restaurants include Abner's in The Soo and the Antlers, a nondescript building housing one of the most unusual eateries you'll ever encounter, including a snake curling up a tree built into the bar. No ski rentals are available in the area. There are casinos in Brimley and The Soo. There's a hospital in The Soo.

Phone numbers: Sault Ste. Marie Ranger District for Hiawatha National Forest, (906) 635–5311. Ojibway Hotel, (906) 632–4100; Abner's, (906) 632–4221. The Antlers, (906) 632–3571. Sault Ste. Marie Convention and Visitors Bureau, (906) 632–3301 or (800) 647–2858; Web site, www.saultstemarie.com.

IN THE FAR EASTERN Upper Peninsula, farmlands have replaced most of the forest that once covered the area, but when there is some, it's made the most of, and such is the case here. The trail is located on a series of ancient Lake Superior (geologists call this glacial-age water body Lake Algonquin) sand dunes. There are some huge hardwoods here, many

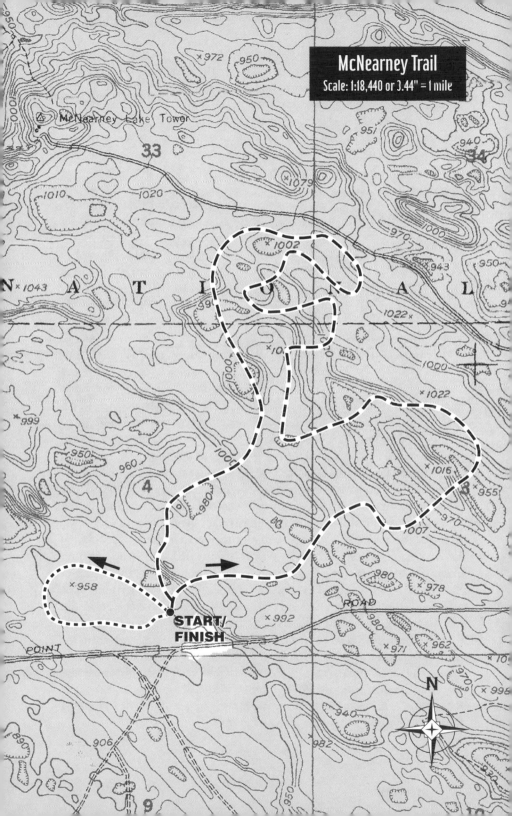

McNearney Trail
Scale: 1:18,440 or 3.44" = 1 mile

START/
FINISH

more than 150 years old. There's also a white spruce plantation through the valleys between the hills. Pull into the parking lot and you're already immersed in some U.P. history. The lot was the site of Camp 4, a turn-of-the-19th-century logging camp that one of the loops is named for.

Beginners can head out from the trailhead on Loop 1, aptly named the Beginner's Loop. It curves off to your left from the lot and will take you in a gentle circle through the surrounding hardwoods to come right back to your vehicle. It's all level and a great scenic area for first-timers.

Directions at a glance

MILE

0.0   From parking lot turn right onto Camp 4 Loop.

0.75 Turn left at intersection.

1.0   Turn left at intersection.

1.25 Continue through intersection.

2.5   Turn right to return to lot.

Camp 4 Loop is also for beginners and low intermediates. From the lot start by heading off to your right. There's a 100-foot uphill climb at first, but once you're at the top of the ridge, it's fairly gentle. On the backside returning to the parking lot, the drop is more gradual. You'll loop constantly to your left until you meet with the more-difficult Big Pine Loop about 1 mile in. Continue to your left and about 0.25 mile later, you'll meet Big Pine's end and the start of Forester's Loop before heading in a gentle arc through the hills and down a straightaway. The trail curves left, then makes a fairly straight run to return to the start.

Forester's Loop is for advanced skiers, because there are several sharp turns and hills up to 100 feet high that will make your lungs burn. The climbs are a bit more gentle than the descents. Look for turns in the downhill side, but the hairpins on the map are generally located on the flats. All the hills come in the middle of the trail, starting immediately after a sharp right turn. The best way to reach it is by heading out onto Camp 4 Loop until the trails intersect. Once you're past the series of hills, the run back to the start of the loop is a gentle, cool-down run with a few short uphill loops. Downhill slopes are relatively easy. From the intersection back to the lot, you'll take a portion of Camp 4 Loop.

Big Pine Loop heads off from Camp 4. Just keep going straight from the intersection and you'll soon be engulfed by large hardwoods that are an estimated 150 years old. In the valleys between the hills are white spruce planted here in the 1960s. There's also a 110-foot-tall white pine that pokes its limbs up high above the forest canopy. If you keep looking for it, you'll see it; otherwise it's easy to miss.

Giant Pines Loop
Tahquamenon Falls State Park, Paradise

Trail type: ▰ ◄ ⬤

> *Note:* Snowshoeing is off piste.

Location: Just off MI 123, 15 miles northeast of Paradise.

Also used by: No one.

Distance: Two loops, 3.7 and 6.6 miles.

Terrain: Slightly rolling, winding through a primeval old-growth hardwood and conifer forest within the park. The largest hills are about 30 feet. You'll also ski up to Michigan's largest waterfall, the famous Tahquamenon Upper Falls. Snowshoers with enough stamina can trek to the lower falls, a series of stair-step-like cataracts.

Trail difficulty: Easiest to more difficult.

Surface quality: Groomed and double track set weekly on Giant Pines Loop. Wilderness Loop is ungroomed, but generally has a skier-set track.

Food and facilities: There are plenty of restaurants in Paradise, a major snowmobile rest stop. Not on park property but within the park is a unique little eatery, the Tahquamenon Falls Brewery & Pub at Camp 33. House-brewed beer and root beer are served. Motels in the Newberry area, southwest of the actual falls, include the Days Inn, with 42 rooms, an indoor pool, and nearby restaurants. There are no ski rentals available. Vault toilets are open at the trailhead. A state park motor-vehicle permit is required to enter; $4.00 daily, $20.00 annually. There are no other trail fees. There's a hospital in Newberry.

Phone numbers: Tahquamenon Falls State Park, (906) 492–3415. Tahquamenon Falls Brewery & Pub, (906) 492–3300. Newberry Chamber of Commerce, (906) 293–3917. Days Inn, (906) 293–4000.

TAHQUAMENON IS ONE of the most storied locations in all the state. The setting for Longfellow's epic *Hiawatha,* the river holds a special place in the hearts of those who visit it because it's so beautiful, especially in winter when visitors are fewest. You'll be skiing through one of the state's premier old-growth northern hardwood forests, with lots of beech, maple, yellow birch, and eastern hemlock, along with a few great old white pines I'll talk about later.

To get to the start of Giant Pines Loop, enter the park on the entrance road. The trail starts right from the parking lot and, for the first leg, follows

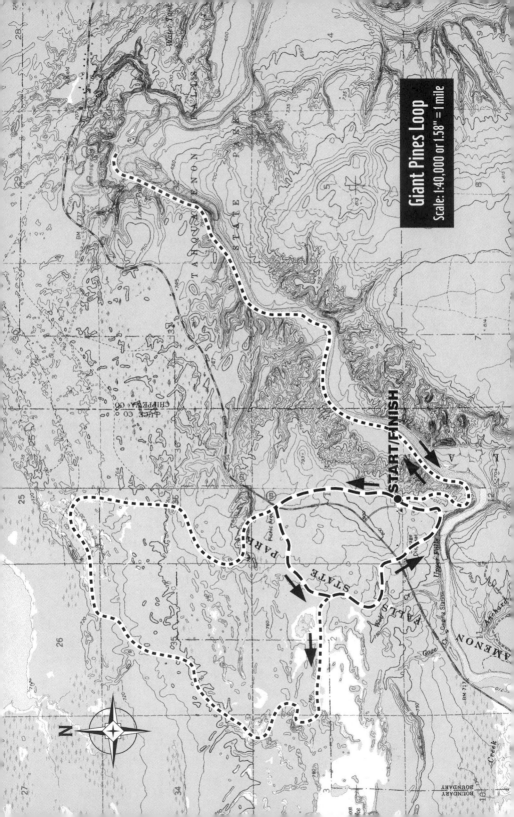

START/FINISH

TAHQUAMENON STATE PARK

CHIPPEWA CO.
LUCE CO.

Water Trail

BM 737

FALLS STATE PARK

Picnic Area

Dist. Hotel

Upper Falls

Gage

Gaging Station

TAHQUAMENON

BOUNDARY

BM 717

Creek

N

the main walking trail down to the falls. This first 0.4-mile segment is packed, but generally walkers have obscured the set track. The falls is one of the largest in the eastern United States, depending on how you measure it. At 50 feet high and 200 across, it's certainly the state's largest, spewing thousands of gallons of tea-colored water—swamp tannins give it this hue—over the brink and onto the ice formations below. The falls is usually encrusted in snow and ice.

From the falls the set track should be in good shape. You'll now be heading northwest. About 0.75 mile in from the falls, you'll cross MI 123 and the snowmobile trail. Usually the road has enough snow cover that you won't have to take off your skis.

Directions at a glance

MILE

0.0 From parking lot head north on Giant Pines Loop.

1.0 Turn left.

1.8 Go south through trail intersection, or take longer Wilderness Loop.

3.7 Return to lot.

From this point you'll soon enter the giant-pines area, namesake of the loop. This is big-tree country, with eastern hemlock making up the majority of what you're seeing. But you will be soon passing a gem: the second largest known white pine in Michigan, a 200-footer that's between 200 and 400 years old.

The trail then loops to your right a bit, where you'll get into the largest hills on the segment: gradual ups and downs over some ancient dune ridges that even beginners will be able to handle.

At the next intersection you've got a chance to head left onto Wilderness Loop, that 6.6-mile ungroomed segment that usually has a track. It's rated more difficult, but mostly for its length and snow depths, not for its terrain.

If you're staying on Giant Pines, continue straight ahead through the dense forest for about 0.8 mile. You'll cross the snowmobile trail again just before MI 123. From that point it's about another mile back to the parking lot on a very flat glide through the forest.

If you opt to take on Wilderness, you'll be going over more rolling hills, but nothing major. You'll leave the hardwoods in favor of red and white pine ridges, black spruce bogs, and swale. Be sure to watch for wildlife, including gray jays, spruce grouse, and boreal chickadees. Toward the end you'll also pass an old unoccupied beaver pond, one of two water bodies you'll see on this loop, both of which will look like openings in the forest. It's a great landmark telling you where you are. A short distance beyond, turn right and head south back to Giant Pines Loop.

A favorite of snowshoers who don't want to walk the ski trail is Tahquamenon River Trail, a 5.5-mile one-way trip (that's 11 miles round trip, remember, unless you spot a car at the lower falls parking lot so you'll have transportation back). It's not recommended for skiers, because there are stairs to climb along with other hazards.

The trail here intermittently leaves and follows the river, but you'll be in a winter wonderland all the way. You won't see much open water, but do not go onto the river ice. The area gets so much snow that there may be 2 to 4 feet on top of the ice. It insulates so well that the ice will actually melt away underneath, leaving a snow bridge that could collapse at any time. The occasional pockets of open water you see are what's left of those snow bridges. The river here is obviously cold and very deep and you're a long way from help. Stay off.

Tahquamenon Falls makes a great photo subject on a winter visit.

The riverbank scenery is also different from the surrounding forest, with lots of white cedar and fir. You stand a chance of seeing otters come and go at the river's edge, along with pine martens, foxes, and coyotes.

Another fun part of skiing Tahquamenon is the restaurant. It's not on park property, but it's inside the park boundary, and its owners are descendants of the folks who sold the land to the state to be used as a park. It gets its name from a former lumber camp, the 33rd camp the logging company was to build. Skiing the park is a unique experience that should be on the must-do list of anyone heading to the U.P.'s trails.

Munising Cross-Country Ski Trail
Pictured Rocks National Lakeshore, Munising

Trail type: ▬▬ ⬤

Note: Snowshoeing is off trail.

Location: Within Pictured Rocks National Lakeshore, approximately a mile from Munising. From town take County Road H-58 east to the first ski-trail parking lot. There is additional parking at the end of East City Limits Road, north of H-58.

Also used by: No one. A snowmobile trail crosses two loops.

Distance: Eight loops totaling 11.7 miles, ranging from 2.4 to 8 miles.

Terrain: Routes go through great stands of hardwoods and glacial moraines. The steepest elevation drops are about 150 feet atop the Pictured Rocks Cliffs. There is only one most-difficult-rated trail, but intermediate terrain has some challenging ups and downs.

Trail difficulty: Easiest to most difficult.

Surface quality: Six trails are groomed twice weekly, others regularly. Parts of three are open to two-way traffic. Trails are groomed for striding only.

Food and facilities: There is an informational kiosk at both parking lots. Trails are free. Restaurants and accommodations are numerous around Munising, the western terminus of the Pictured Rocks. Accommodations include the Best Western 3 miles east of town along MI 28. It has 80 rooms with an indoor pool and restaurant. Restaurants in town include Dogpatch, serving breakfast, lunch, and dinner. Don't judge it by its quirky name; it's good. Ski rentals are available at Wheels in Munising. There's a hospital in Munising.

Phone numbers: Pictured Rocks National Lakeshore, (906) 387–3700. Best Western, (906) 387–4864. Dogpatch, (906) 387–9948. Wheels, (906), 387–6900 or (877) 387–2925.

YOU MAY NEVER find a more picturesque place to ski than here along the lip of a natural sandstone rock face plunging into Lake Superior. All loops but one require intermediate ski experience at most, so practically anyone can come and enjoy the magnificent scenery that these cliffs shaped by wind, rain, ice, and time hold. The trails wind through a beautiful landscape of beech, maple, hemlock, spruce, and old fields on sandy uplands and hills of glacial moraines. From the lower parking lot off County Road H-58, Trail A—a 2.4-mile run rated easiest—begins by

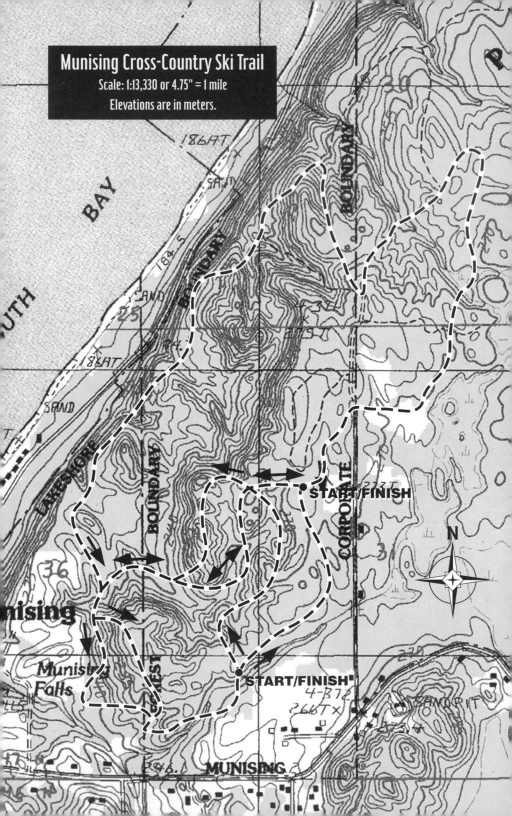

Munising Cross-Country Ski Trail
Scale: 1:13,330 or 4.75" = 1 mile
Elevations are in meters.

START/FINISH

START/FINISH

Munising
Falls

MUNISING

N

heading off to your right, skirting the hardwood and hemlock hills.

Only a few hundred yards in, you'll be deep into the woods and encountering the first intersection, with Trail B. This is a 1.9-mile trek that's the only one in the system rated most difficult. You'll find drops of up to 150 feet spread over hills extending about 100 yards in distance, some with sharp turns at the bottom, slopes of about 20 percent, and vertical drops of 150 feet. B runs counterclockwise, and right where it bends west—and where it first meets, then slips below, Trail A—is one of those hills. The intersection of A and B is marked by blue diamonds, which are placed at each intersection. Trail A continues to your right. Take it, and about 0.5 mile later you'll make the first crossing of the snowmobile trail that skirts the area. Where the lower part of A enters a field, you'll be treated to some great views of the lake.

The easiest way to get to Trail H, an intermediate glide and probably the most scenic, is to start at the City Limits Road parking lot. You'll want to either head left onto Trail E or take a portion of C rated more difficult. C starts with a good 100-foot hill that handles two-way traffic, so be cautious on this segment. E is a 0.8-mile easiest-rated run. At the intersection of Trails E and F, turn left and continue on F, a 1.7-mile intermediate route. It intersects with H, which heads southwest, and you'll soon be staring over those famous timber-covered sandstone cliffs that make the 18-mile-long lakeshore one of the state's and nation's natural wonders. Stains on the rock are formed as minerals leach though the soil and run down the rock face. The sight of icy Superior sloshing against the rock wall or, depending on the day, locked in white is something you'll not forget. Other grand sights are the several frozen waterfalls you'll see in a number of spots along H.

Directions at a glance

MILE

0.0 From south lot head north on Trail A.

1.5 Turn left and continue on A.

1.9 Go through intersection on A.

2.5 Continue through intersection on A.

3.0 Continue through intersection on A.

3.1 Continue through intersection on A.

4.0 Return to lot.

Trail H bobs and weaves along the bluff, where you'll encounter undulating hills up to 150 feet high, one or two with straight runouts. Expect to get up some good speed. You'll also find some equally interesting climbs of the same height. There are some sharp turns at the ends of a few of those downhills, too, including the point where H

A GUIDED U.P. ADVENTURE

L ooking for an easy way to explore the U.P. in winter? Rah Trost has the answer. The founder of Marquette's Great Northern Adventures takes folks on guided ski, snowshoe, and even dogsled treks throughout the winter and even in summer.

You won't be roughing it on her trips. A two-day, two-night trip into the Pictured Rocks National Lakeshore on either skis or snowshoes includes meals, two nights' lodging, and guide service. This trip is for beginning and intermediate skiers, but Trost can cook up a journey for anyone. There are also one-day tours and inn-to-inn samplers as long as seven days. Snowshoers can also pick a special two-day trip to see the U.P. wilderness.

Dogsled adventures explore trails through the Hiawatha National Forest. You can choose from rustic cabin lodgings or lodge-based tours. Reach Trost by calling (906) 225-TOUR, or via the Internet at http://greatnorthernadventures. com. Equipment rental and all-women tours are also available.

quickly turns left away from the bluffs and meets up with Trails A and B. Turn right here onto either track for the short trek across the snowmobile trail and back to the lot. You needn't worry too much about running into snowmobiles, because trails here don't get much traffic. One word of caution on this system: Even though tracks like F and G are rated easiest or more difficult, total mileage also figures in. Because these loops are all connected and you must travel one distance to get to another, make sure you can handle not only the hills but the miles, too.

Valley Spur Ski Trails
Hiawatha National Forest, Munising

Trail type: ═══ ◄ ⬤⬤⬤

Notes: Single tracked with separate runs set aside for skaters, although most would also accommodate a skater and a strider side by side. No snowshoes are allowed on ski trails, off piste recommended only with a GPS.

Location: Just off MI 94, approximately 4 miles south of Munising. From MI 28 turn south onto MI 94 and go about 4 miles. Watch for the VALLEY SPUR sign on your right, and turn left opposite it. There is a secondary parking lot just to the south.

Also used by: No one. The complex is a mountain biking area in warm weather. A portion of the national North Country Hiking Trail goes by the complex.

Distance: 38 miles of trails forming interconnected loops, ranging from 0.9 to 7 miles. There are four skating loops totaling 14 miles. Distances are measured as round trips starting from and returning to the lodge. All trails are marked starting at the lodge; at each junction you'll find signs and at least one map showing where you are.

Terrain: Trails are located in a thick mixed hardwood and pine tract, part of the Hiawatha National Forest. More-difficult runs are at slightly higher elevations. Most-difficult trails have lots of steeps to challenge you. Elevation changes on beginner runs are slight but on more experienced trails range up to 200 feet, so prepare to be thrilled on the way down.

Trail difficulty: Easiest to most difficult.

Surface quality: Both skating and traditional trails are groomed regularly. Traditional are single track set and feature very wide lanes, so skating or traditional skiing friends could probably ski alongside.

Food and facilities: The trail is so popular there's a day lodge open on weekends usually from 10:00 A.M. until dusk, with one pit toilet, heated on weekends. The suggested donation of $5.00 goes directly into grooming. Skis are sometimes available for rental on weekends at the trailhead lodge. Restaurants in downtown Munising include Dogpatch, an eclectic place downtown just off MI 28 serving breakfast through dinner. Lodging can be found along MI 28 near Munising, including the Best Western, which has an indoor pool and whirlpool. In downtown Munising, limited ski rentals are available at Wheels. There's a hospital in Munising.

Phone numbers: U.S. Forest Service office, Munising Ranger District, (906) 387–2512. Valley Spur lodge (weekends), (906) 387–4918. Wheels, (906) 387–5900. Dogpatch, (906) 387–9948. Munising Best Western, (906) 387–4864. For other information contact the Alger County Chamber of Commerce in Munising, (906) 387–2138.

THIS IS ONE of the most popular trail systems in Michigan's vast Upper Peninsula, and once you arrive, you'll easily see why. The system has a great variety of trails for all ability levels, from moderate-length or short jaunts for beginners to longies for skaters who want to stretch their legs and endurance. An estimated 2,000 to 4,000 skiers per season use the loops.

A large log warming lodge is staffed on weekends (hot drinks are often available) and has plenty of chairs in which to relax and wait for your friends still on the trail.

From the main parking lot, trails leave to your right of the lodge, while the first skating loop trail, X, heads out from midway in the parking lot a bit south of the lodge. I sampled two trails and part of a third.

Loop A is a great warm-up or beginner run. Starting from the lodge, it climbs a low-elevation incline that gets steeper later, but not before A turns off to your right. A, in fact, brings most skiers to the rest of the trails. There it begins to curl around the base of the hills that form a plateau for many of the runs higher up. You'll get a taste of what the surrounding forestland is like—a tremendous mix of beeches, maples, a few white pines and spruces.

A turns sharply right, bordering the base of several hills holding the

Directions at a glance

MILE

0.0   Enter trail system next to warming cabin and stay on Loop B.

1.0   Veer to right to stay on B.

2.0   Jog right or stay on main trail to return to lot.

See trail map for information on other loops.

runs higher up. It then begins a steady, gentle downhill run toward the lot, curving in a series of esses and finally meeting up with lower portions of skater trails at the last intersection before the parking lot.

Loop B is one of the most picturesque beginner runs you'll find anywhere in the state. It gives plenty of time and distance—2.8 miles' worth—to practice. After leaving from the lodge area on a hard left, it wanders through heavy woods, weaving a delightful journey along the base of yet more hills. It includes a long straightaway nicknamed Locomotive Chase, a reference to the ski complex's moniker, which came

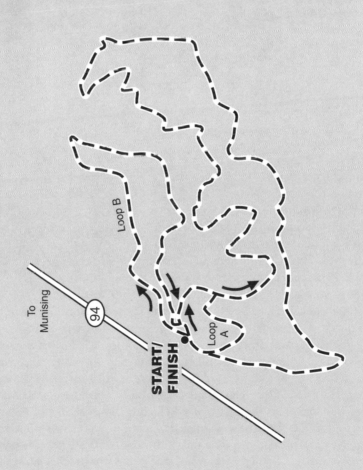

Valley Spur Ski Trails
No scale map available for this trail

N

To
Munising

94

START/
FINISH

Loop B

Loop
A

Skiers leave the rustic lodge that replaced an old trailer a few years ago.

from the old logging railroad grade that Loop B passes. You'll also pass a pond, cross Valley Spur Creek four times, and go through a magnificent old-growth hemlock grove with some hardwoods on either side. There are some hills, but the runouts are straight. It's probably the most popular route in the system. When you meet the start of the 1.6-mile most-difficult H loop, you're about halfway through your journey on B. It meets H's exit a few hundred yards later, then peels off on a mostly gentle, controllable downhill run back to the base.

Intermediates looking for a challenge can leave from the staging area. At the first intersection Loops D, E (an advanced trail), and F (for more experienced) head off to your right, while Loop C runs off to your left. Loop C is a shorty at 1.4 miles, but worthy of its advanced status, because it's technically very difficult. A series of short, downhill slopes range from 16 to 20 percent grades. Because of turns in midtrail and those compressions, plus the fact that you'll climb from a base of 620 feet to the top at 950 feet, it has earned its most-difficult status. One stretch, Stairway to Heaven, is a long uphill through an old glacial valley that's not too difficult if you stop to rest. Once you get to the plateau at the top, you're rewarded with a beautiful sight of huge stands of beech, sugar and red maple, and birch. Take a look at some of the trailside trees, especially the birch. You'll see some curious marks, as if someone with a four-bladed knife had marked their trunks at various intervals. Black bears that apparently love to stretch their legs climb here after nuts in late spring and fall. You needn't worry about them in winter.

Loops E, F, and G are all most difficult trails that play along the same ridgeline you'll see from below. Each basically comes back soon, with G the farthest out. Slopes range up to a 20 percent grade and are designed and groomed for better skiers. Hills are all "front-half loaded," meaning that the most difficult are in the first half so you can rest as you return, when you're up on the elevated flats. Those flats provide good kick-and-glide areas where you can practice and pick up your rhythm. Some of the downhill runs, however, are straight, and some require you to turn while headed downhill, to negotiate banked turns that are often untracked. It's a little hairy, but rewarding.

Skating trails fan out a little like a butterfly on the trail map. The shortest is Loop X at 1.8 miles, which parallels Loop C. Aside from the fact that you've got to get up that same long, steep slope (not the same trail, though; it carries a steeper angle), it's fairly easy skating once you're at the top. W is simply an extension of X and is a good loop to work on your technique, because it's fairly level with small hills.

Loop Y, on the other hand, is for someone who wants to go the distance. At 7 miles it's the longest of them all, but fairly level. There is a spot where you must climb the same ridge to get to the top plateau as the other trails, but aside from that, Loop Y is considered by those who ski it regularly as probably the best for working on your skating technique and rhythm. Loop Z, on the other hand, is all hill. Up to the point where Y goes right and Z left, it's flat, but right afterward it's ready to take you on, and it doesn't stop going up and down until it joins with X for the trip back home.

Harlow Lake Ski Trail
Little Presque Isle State Forest Recreation Area, Marquette

Trail type: ▬▬ ▬ ⬮⬮⬮

Note: There's an ungroomed but well-marked trail leaving from the gravel pit. From the cabins you can also head out to break trail or follow another skier's tracks around the lake. Check locally for ice thickness before attempting to cross the lake. Head south along the shore to eventually meet up with the ski trail. Snowshoers can trek up a nearby mountain as well.

Location: In the Little Presque Isle Tract, part of the Little Presque Isle State Forest Recreation Area, off Marquette County Road 550, approximately 4 miles north of the Marquette city limits. Follow the signs to Big Bay from MI 28/U.S. 41. Turn north onto McClellan, then east onto Fair. Turn north onto Lincoln and follow it past Northern Michigan University's campus while continuing to watch for the signs directing you to Big Bay at intersections. Turn east onto Wright and north onto Sugar Loaf, which connects with County Road 550. On 550 you'll pass the 550 Store, where trail information is available. There are two access points. The main parking lot is to your left off County Road 550 at an area known as Clark's Gravel Pit. Or you can continue north to a small road leading to the cabins along Harlow Lake. Turn left into the access road just before Harlow Lake and park in the small lot.

Also used by: One section takes in part of a dogsled trail. Otherwise, there's no one here but skiers and snowshoers.

Distance: Approximately 6 miles.

Terrain: Heavily wooded countryside with a steady but easily managed uphill grade totaling about 150 feet.

Trail difficulty: More difficult to most difficult.

Surface quality: Groomed and/or skier-set tracks. Snowshoers can walk alongside the tracks or head cross-country. Taking a compass and/or GPS is strongly advised.

Food and facilities: Ski fees are by donation at the trailhead. Restaurants are available in Marquette, including the Vierling Restaurant & Marquette Harbor Brewery at 119 South Front downtown, and the Northwoods Supper Club, 3.5 miles west on U.S. 41/MI 28, then 0.3 mile south at the sign. Accommodations include the Days Inn a mile or so west of McClellan at 2403

West U.S. 41/MI 28, with 65 rooms, an indoor pool, adjacent restaurant, and ski storage and waxing room. Comfort Suites is right next door. The Tiroler Hof Inn on a hill overlooking Marquette's harbor at 1880 U.S. 41/MI 28 south of downtown has 44 rooms; the historic 1930s-era Landmark Inn downtown has 62 rooms. Several shops in Marquette rent or sell and tune skis. Ski rentals are also available from the gymnasium complex of Northern Michigan University, next to the Yooperdome in Marquette, the world's largest wooden-domed stadium. Check with the convention and visitors bureau for information. There's a hospital in Marquette.

Phone numbers: Department of Natural Resources, Ishpeming field office, (906) 485–1031. Trail and cabin rental information is available at the 550 Store along County Road 550 and Middle Island Point Road, 2 miles from the intersection of Wright Street and Sugar Loaf Avenue, and about 4 miles south of Harlow Lake Road. The store is on the northern side of the road. Days Inn, (906) 225–1393. Comfort Suites, (906) 228–0028. Vierling Restaurant & Marquette Harbor Brewery, (906) 228–3533. Northwoods Supper Club, (906) 228–4343. Tiroler Hof Inn, (906) 226–7516. Landmark Inn, (906) 228–2580. Marquette Country Convention and Visitors Bureau, (800) 544–2341; Web site, www.marquettecountry.org.

THIS LITTLE SKI hideaway is a great find that's generally used only by locals. It's in a beautiful backcountry setting only a few miles outside the Upper Peninsula's largest city, and takes in some of the most scenic, hilliest country in the U.P. The tract itself is 3,040 acres; most was owned by a local family until ending up in state control.

Our visit began alongside 64-acre Harlow Lake, next to one of five lakeside cabins built by the state that skiers or hikers may rent. The log structures have wood-burning stoves and bunk beds and sleep up to six. It was early February, and we knew the ice was safe to cross to the lake's southeastern side. We broke trail through the trees along the shore, heading south, until eventually we met up with the regular ski trail that starts from the gravel pit area.

We then turned right onto the trail leading us away from the lake and began a long, constant, but gradual incline through deep woods and along ravines and other areas that made not only beautiful stopping points to catch our breath but also perfect wildlife cover. We did not see any of the area's deer or other animals on our trip.

Eventually the trail wandered through the woods and curved to the south, where we crossed a county road used in winter as a ski and

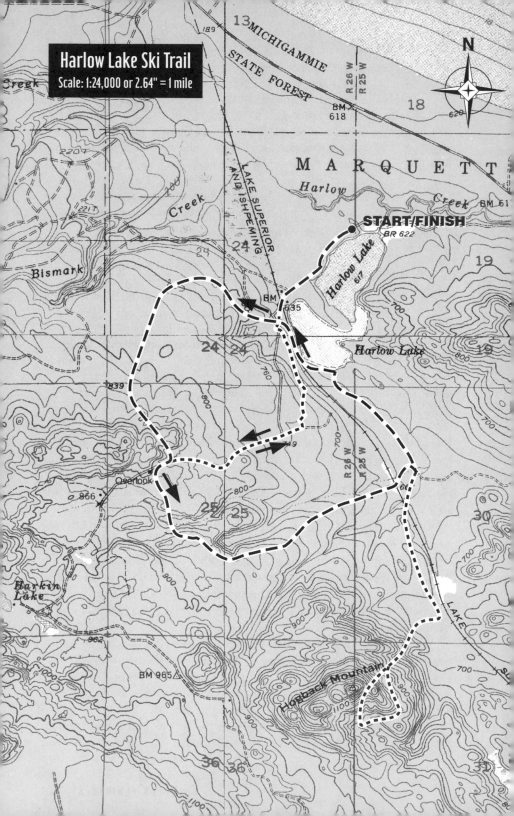

Directions at a glance

MILE

0.0   From cabins break trail on western side of lake. Head south.

0.5   Meet tracked trail at southwestern end of lake.

1.5   Cross dogsled trail and continue to overlook.

1.6   Head east on dogsled trail downhill back toward lake.

2.5   Return to lake and cabins.

dogsled trail. About 20 feet above us through the trees, the trees cleared at the point some locals call Eagle's Knob. We herringboned and side-stepped up the last steep 30 feet and stood upon this majestic promontory looking over a rocky cliff for a spectacular view of the Huron Mountains— these hills are the start of the chain that runs west to the Keweenaw Peninsula—a brooding Lake Superior to the east beyond the trees, and Sugar Loaf Mountain, an 1,100-foot-high Marquette landmark.

Since the descent from the overlook is very steep and treed, you'll probably want to take off your skis and gingerly step down to the wide, open trail that's really an unplowed road. From there you'll be rewarded for all your hard work with a restful, nearly all downhill run back to lake level through some of the most beautiful and quiet stands of northern hard-

A snowshoer tackles the Harlow Lake Trail.

woods you'll ever see. It's a great way to cool down after your climb, and it's an easy ski. Our party of three never saw another skier on this route, a good indication that your trip, too, will introduce you to a bit of U.P. solitude.

The snowshoers in our party meanwhile headed south from the lake and up along the trail to Hogback Mountain, 600 feet above Harlow Lake via a spectacular hiking trail that rewards 'shoers with wonderful views of Lake Superior and the Huron Mountains, much as does Eagle's Knob. If you're in fairly good condition, you won't find the trek too strenuous.

One good way to see the trails is to reserve a cabin for the day, leave your lunch and other equipment there, enjoy your walk or ski, and return to start a fire and either cook a hot meal or buy some pasties—the local U.P. delicacy—for lunch. Pasties, for the uninitiated, are enclosed meat pies made with beef or all vegetables, but particularly with rutabagas. Combined with your right spices, that veggie gives them a unique taste. They were a staple of copper and iron miners, and you'll see pasty shops everywhere. A U.P. ski is not complete without trying at least one.

Blueberry Ridge Pathway

Escanaba River State Forest, Marquette

Trail type: ━━ ◄

Location: In the Escanaba River State Forest, about 6 miles south of Marquette. From MI 28/U.S. 41, take McClellan Avenue south. It becomes County Road 553 until just past the intersection with County Road 480. The parking lot is on the eastern side of the road.

Notes: Skating and striding are allowed on three trails, traditional skiing only on three. There's one lighted trail. All trails are one-way, with skiers heading clockwise.

Distance: Seven loops totaling 20 kilometers.

Terrain: This is a heavily wooded trail through beautiful hills and meadows only a few miles south of Marquette. It can be hilly at times, with climb to the Superior Loop overlook from the lowest part of the trail from a canyon up to the overlook, about 300 feet.

Trail difficulty: Easiest to most difficult.

Surface quality: Groomed regularly. Traditional loops are double tracked. Skating loops are single tracked.

Food and facilities: See Harlow Lake Trail for Marquette-area restaurants and accommodations. The Crossroads Bar and Restaurant is across the street from one of the trailheads. Rentals are available in Marquette at Down Wind Sports, 14 North Third Street, or in Ishpeming at Maple Lane Sports, 1015 Country Lane. Down Wind also rents snowshoes. Unisex bathrooms are found at each parking lot. No drinking water is available. Fees are collected by donation at the trailhead. Marquette Mountain downhill ski area is also nearby for telemarkers. There's a hospital in Marquette.

Phone numbers: Department of Natural Resources, Marquette office, (906) 249–1497. Free area trail maps are available from the Marquette Country Convention and Visitors Bureau, (800) 544–2341; Web site, www.marquettecountry.org. Maple Lane Sports, (906) 485–1636. Down Wind Sports, (906) 226–7112. Marquette Mountain, (906) 225–1155 or (800) 944–7669.

ONE OF MICHIGAN'S most varied and picturesque trail systems lies in the red and jack pine forests only a few minutes south of the Upper Peninsula's largest city. It has the bumps for advanced skiers and the flats for begin-

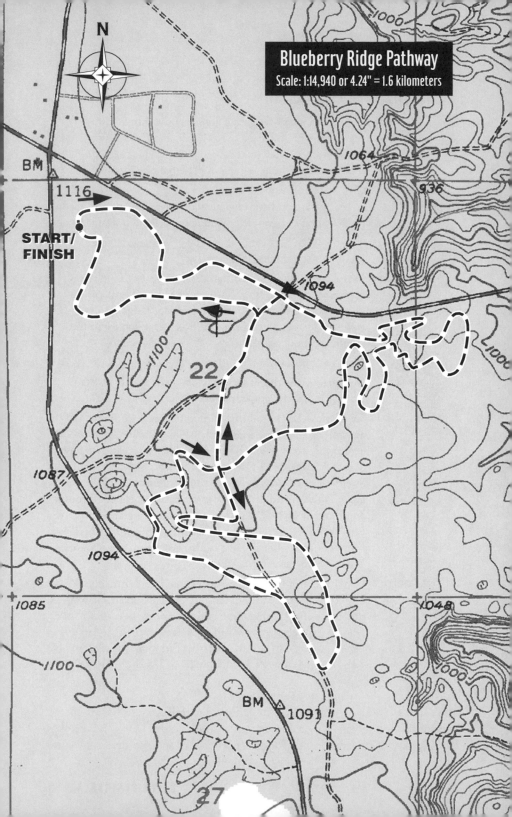

ners, with plenty of scenery to please everyone, including a trail that's lighted every night of the season. Weekends may find the parking lot jammed, so you may have to leave your car on County Road 553.

There are two parking lot access points. At the northern end are two great loops for intermediate and beginner skiers.

From the lot the easiest loop is Crossroads, at 2.4 kilometers a great distance for starters. Enter the trail and you're on mostly flats as the route heads north, then generally east through pine and stands of mixed timber, with few if any hills the entire way back to the lot. Combining this with the more-difficult Husky Loop is probably the most popular route. Together they total 4.8 kilometers.

Instead of turning right onto the home leg of Crossroads, you'll go straight to get to Husky. Shortly after you make the separation, you'll start encountering short downhill runs of 20 feet, which you can cruise without too much effort. You'll go over a knob with a little steeper downhill of 20 to 30 feet just before intersecting with the entrance to the most-difficult-rated Spartan Loop.

Continue on Husky and you'll run into more undulating terrain as you head south, with one good drop of about 25 feet in about 75 yards. Just before you merge with the more-difficult Wolverine Loop, there's one good climb of about 50 feet. Husky then loops back to the north on its way to meet with Crossroads through mostly flat country and a jack pine forest. The last 1 kilometer has a couple of easy 20-foot downhill glides.

Spartan is the most entertaining of the three northern loops. It's rated most difficult, but if you're a good intermediate or a beginner who wants to push the envelope a bit, it's for you. It's a roller-coaster ride of ups and downs averaging 15 feet through its entire 2.6 kilometers, one that doesn't leave you alone for the entire ride.

Turn onto the loop and about 0.5 kilometer later, you'll reach a good 25-foot stair-step downhill in legs of about 10 and 15 feet between a brief flat. Twisting like a big noodle, the trail finally heads south then west through a series of turns to finish with a nice 20-foot downhill and an uphill turn to tie back in with Husky Loop.

It's a true treat to ski a well-lighted loop, and Blueberry is one of the best in the state. Streetlights installed by the city Board of Light and

Directions at a glance

KILOMETER	
0.0	From north lot enter trail from left.
0.75	Turn right at marker 2 or continue through to rest of system.
1.25	Turn right at intersection.
1.5	Return to lot.

Power, the State Department of Natural Resources, and the Superiorland Ski Club are illuminated nightly. Don't worry about shadowy hills, because this trail is rated easiest. It follows, in part, the path of Old County Road 553, and also takes in some of the system's dedicated skating loop. From the parking lot go north, then east for about 100 yards before you split from Wolverine Loop. You'll then head south for about 1 kilometer before you tie back in to Wolverine for a bit, then head south back to the parking lot.

From that parking lot you can also access Wolverine, a mostly intermediate trek. A short stride from the parking lot is the hill known as the Wolverine Slide, a 50- to 75-foot drop that's an eye-watering experience even for experts. If it's icy, you'll be doing about 30 miles per hour at the bottom, but it's a nice straight runout. After that you'll encounter a steady climb and immediately enter a beautiful red pine forest for the balance of your stay on Wolverine. Here are more undulating 20-foot ups and downs, but the trail skis very well and eventually bends back to the lighted loop for about the last 1 kilometer. Wolverine is 4.3 kilometers long.

Blueberry Ridge routes suit all ages.

Next up is Superior Loop, at 4.6 kilometers. It's a very nice most-difficult trail with lots of undulating terrain. Advanced skiers will learn a lot about using edges and keeping momentum going.

As soon as you enter the loop—within the first 75 yards or so—you'll turn left onto a good 30-foot drop. You'll need to take this at pretty good speed, balance, and quite a bit of articulation to get around the corner at the bottom.

Following that are a couple of more turns and two drops, the first a 20-footer. Then there's a climb, and next a plunge known as the Elevator, a steep descent of about 25 feet that develops some good g-forces. You'll bottom out in a pothole.

A bit later on you'll go through one more 50-foot drop with a straight runout and several more 20- to 30-foot bumps. Stay on Superior and you'll be heading back to the lot along the rim of what's locally known as the Canyon, a 200-foot furrow looming below you through the trees. About 0.5 kilometer from where Superior turns sharply back is Lookout Point, where on a clear day you'll be able to see a good 20 miles to the east over the forest. There's also a bench where you can rest and picnic. Past the rest stop the trail drops a bit, then climbs slowly but steadily about 75 feet back to the start.

Finally, Wildcat, at 2.7 kilometers, is a neat most-difficult trail still being developed in an area that has been logged off. It's generally not until the first of the year that there's enough snow to groom it properly. It partly follows an old road, so it's wide. But it has also got a lot of pretty turns and twists with 15- to 20-foot drops until it eventually sinks into that canyon your friends are looking at from above on Superior via a part of the rail called Luge Run, a 200-foot-plus downhill drop on an old two-track road that makes for an interesting if not-too-restful trek. By the time you're reunited with Superior Loop, you've regained about 200 feet of elevation and experienced what's obviously the best workout on the entire system.

Rapid River National Cross-Country Ski Trail

Hiawatha National Forest, Rapid River

Trail type: ▭▬ ◁ ▦

Notes: Most trails are unidirectional, with some two-way shortcuts. No snowshoes are allowed on the tracks.

Location: Rapid River, 7 miles north of town along U.S. 41 within the Hiawatha National Forest. Look for the sign, short access road, and a parking lot on the western side of U.S. 41.

Also used by: The occasional deer and bear.

Distance: Taking into account that nearly every trail uses some segment of another, there's a total of 39.2 miles, if you ski each individually. They're divided into seven loops, including 7.4-mile and 4.7-mile dedicated skating routes. Trail location markers and maps are located at each intersection.

Terrain: A variety, from steep pine ridges to flats heavily covered with birch, beech, aspen, and spruce. Depending on the loop, the terrain ranges from flat or nearly flat to steeps that are a challenge even for the most advanced. All trails roughly parallel each other from north to south.

Trail difficulty: Easiest to most difficult.

Surface quality: Groomed and packed regularly. Single track set, but Tot Loop is double tracked. Most trails are unidirectional, so follow each properly. One shortcut trail is used by both striders and skaters. Most trails are wide enough for two skiers abreast, although some spots wind tightly through the forest. The elevation change exceeds 50 feet.

Food and facilities: There's a bulletin board with maps, a resting bench, and outdoor toilets at the trailhead in the parking lot. No water is available at the site. Accommodations include the Best Western Pioneer Inn, with 72 rooms and an indoor pool. There are lots of other options nearby, mostly along U.S. 2 in Rapid River and Escanaba. There are lots of restaurants, too, including Dobbers, a mostly take-out establishment selling that U.P. staple, pasties, in both meat and veggie styles. Voluntary donations at a collection pipe. Rental equipment is available at Brampton Bike & Ski in Gladstone and in Escanaba at Mr. Bike Ski and Fitness. There's a hospital in Escanaba.

Phone numbers: Rapid River Forest Ranger office, located a few miles east of the intersection of U.S. 41 and U.S. 2, (906) 474–6442. Best Western Pioneer Inn, (906) 786–0602. Brampton Bike & Ski, (906) 428–2135. Mr. Bike Ski and Fitness, (906) 786–1200. Dobbers restaurant, (906) 786–0222. Delta County Chamber of Commerce, (906) 786–2192 or (888) 335–8264; Web site: www.DeltaMi.org.

WHAT A NAME!—and one that indicates what an excellent experience awaits you here. Chosen because of its location in a national forest, the trail system offers five loops for traditional Nordic pursuits, along with two for skaters. It's one of the most beautiful and well marked in the Upper Peninsula as it winds through pine-covered dune ridges that probably were once lakefront when Lake Michigan was much higher. It's a treat to have this system in Michigan.

Parents with kids can take them on the aptly named Tot Loop, the shortest and easiest segment. Starting right next to the signage, the 1.2-mile Tot Loop turns right from the parking lot. You're almost immediately engulfed in forest. Huge birch and clumps of spruce greet you as the trail curves back and forth gently for 0.8 mile out. Part of the route then turns straight down a cleared-away gas pipeline, up and down short hills, past a pine plantation, and then reenters the forest to your left at another pipeline marker. You'll ski past a corridor of low balsam, curving around and through the heavy cover as the forest opens and closes around you. The trail meets up with Loop A, with which it piggybacks a bit to add to its mileage back to the lot. Loop A then continues on straight, while Tot Loop heads off to your left (there's a resting bench at the intersection). Once past more aspen, balsam, spruce, and a few burned or cut-over stumps, you're back at the lot 0.4 mile later. The climb and downhill total about 20 vertical feet.

The 0.6-mile shortcut trail on the map is actually part of the skating loop that both striders and skaters can use.

You're in for a nice ride when you take on this trail.

Loop A, meanwhile, keeps going south through the woods. This 2.7-mile segment covers relatively flat terrain that's excellent for beginners or those wanting an easy workout. From the shortcut loop leaving from the lot next to Tot Loop, you'll begin to see why this system is so popular. Its sheer variety in such a compact package is amazing. You can set off directly on others—Loops B and S1 and S2 (both for skaters)—by using this wide trail.

Go left from the lot and follow the well-placed signs. You'll journey through a tall pine forest, passing "bearing trees," used as surveyor's markers. The trail makes several gentle turns through birch and pine, then goes up a slight incline to your left into another pine plantation. It curves up a short hill before the next intersection. S1, a 4.7-mile intermediate-level skating loop, and B, a 6.8-mile more-advanced run so designated for its length, continue straight. Loop A launches into the dense undergrowth to your left. It shuttles through beautiful country, undulating over short drops through the forest, passing burned stumps, dense growth, and open areas and narrowing in spots to near-shoulder-width for about 0.5 mile before intersecting with B for the 0.5-mile journey back to the lot.

From Shortcut Loop, S1 sets off to your right, climbing about 30 feet over short hills through pine, balsam, and aspen into heavy pine and up a 30-foot hill. S1 goes to your right and Loop B heads off to your left to border stands of balsam. S1 meanders up and down short hills through more pine and aspen, then through a stand of stunted pine and up a short 30-foot hill to your left to follow a sand ridge above a series of low bogs. It zigzags for 2.4 miles before meeting Loop B again. S2 is a 7.4-mile chest-buster built in 1993 and rated more advanced because of its length and the sharp elevation changes at the southern end of the complex, where it climbs, then comes off sharp drops of up to 50 feet.

Need a challenge? Head to the farthest loop, D. A 10-mile breath-catcher, it's rated most difficult and should be approached with caution by everyone. Its length, coupled with steep climbs and downhill slopes exceeding 50 feet in elevation

Directions at a glance

MILE

0.0   Enter Loop A at sign.

0.8   Continue straight at intersection.

1.7   Turn left and follow sign at intersection.

2.1   Turn left at intersection.

2.6   Turn left at intersection to return to lot.

over the 3.4-mile segment farthest from the lot, make this one what advanced skiers look for. On the home stretch skiers can take either a part of the more-difficult Loop B, or C and the shortcut loop back to the lot.

In short, it's a wonderful system that's within minutes of your motel—and its whirlpool.

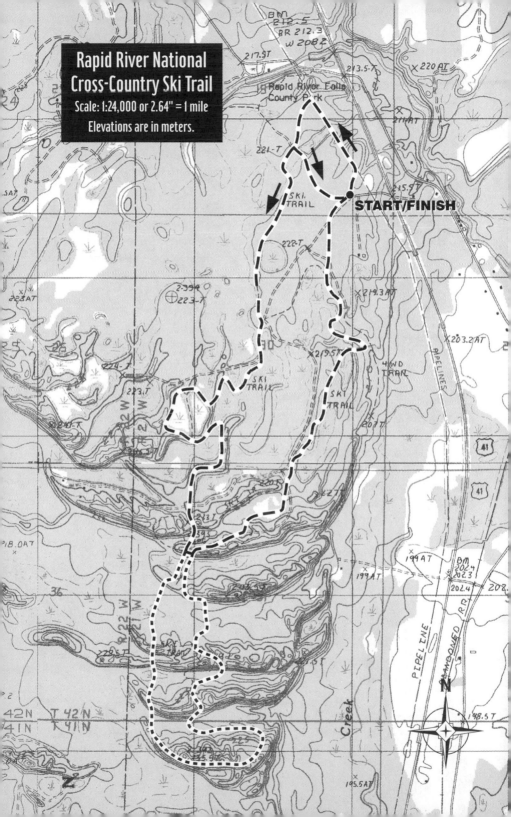

Rapid River National Cross-Country Ski Trail

Scale: 1:24,000 or 2.64" = 1 mile
Elevations are in meters.

START/FINISH

Porcupine Mountains Wilderness State Park Trails

Porcupine Mountains Wilderness State Park, Ontonagon

Trail type: ▬ ◄ ▦

Notes: Trail uses include guided snowshoe hikes and nighttime guided skiing trips. There are elevation changes of up to 700 feet from the lowest loops to the highest. The bulk of the trails, however, boast a maximum elevation change of about 400 feet.

Location: Off MI 107, at 412 South Boundary Road, approximately 13 miles west of Ontonagon.

Also used by: Snowmobile trails do run from the park lodge westward, and one trail parallels the snowmobile route for about 2 kilometers. Another snowmobile trail crosses a more difficult trail on the park's eastern side twice.

Distance: 42 kilometers on six connected scenic loops encircling the lift-served alpine skiing area.

Terrain: Rugged, Upper Peninsula wilderness with beautiful, semi-mountainous scenery. Trails generally meander around the downhill ski area. Some, however, go into the park's interior.

Trail difficulty: Easiest to most difficult.

Surface quality: All trails are power-tilled and double track set, with some skating trails. Check at the ski lodge for skating lane locations.

Food and facilities: Trails lead from the downhill ski lodge, which offers cafeteria service, ski tuning and rental, and free detailed trail maps. In addition there are two trailside warming huts and rustic cabins in the park's interior that can be rented on a reservation basis. Motels nearby include the Best Western Porcupine Mountain Lodge, with 71 rooms, an indoor pool, and a restaurant. Other motels are in Ontonagon. A state park vehicle-entry permit, $4.00 daily or $20.00 annually, is required. Trail fees for ages 18 to 64 run $6.00 daily weekdays, $8.00 weekends; ages 13 to 17 and 65 and over, $3.00 weekdays, $5.00 weekends; children 12 years old and under are free. Your pass includes lift service to the summit of the alpine area with easy access to the heart of the trail system. Trailside cabins rent for $35.00 to $45.00 per night. Ski rentals run $18.00 daily for adults, $13.00 for children 12 and under. Snowshoe rental runs $18.00 daily. There's a hospital in Ontonagon.

Phone numbers: Porcupine Mountains Wilderness State Park, (906) 885–5275. Best Western Porcupine Mountain Lodge, (906) 885–5311. Ontonagon Chamber of Commerce, (906) 884–4735.

THE UPPER PENINSULA is wilderness central for Michigan, and you're in the heart of that capital when you step into your skis here. Within the park's 58,000 acres is one of the largest expanses of virgin northern hemlock west of the Adirondack Mountains, and the highest mountain range in the Midwest. It's about as close to a mountain experience as most midwesterners will find in winter. The drive here may be long, but the rewards are many. And because of the interpretive activities taking place all winter, it's one of the state's most skier- and snowshoer-friendly parks.

Get your bearings at the lodge. If you're comfortable on your skis, head up to the top of the downhill area on a chairlift. But first you owe it to yourself to make the 1-kilometer trek to the West Vista Overlook to get an idea of where you are. You'll be treated to an incomparable view of the cascading countryside as it falls off to the Carp River Valley below you, as well as icy Lake Superior beyond to your north. The East Vista viewing area at the other side of the downhill runs is reached along the more-difficult-rated Log Camp Loop, reached after a 300-foot drop over a 1-kilometer distance into the trail off the back of the downhill area. It sits on the shoulder of the mountain and has some exquisite views into the lake and the Union Bay area—and usually great snow conditions. Then it's time for your first test. Dump down the side for a couple of free

Great vistas await at Porcupine Mountains State Park.

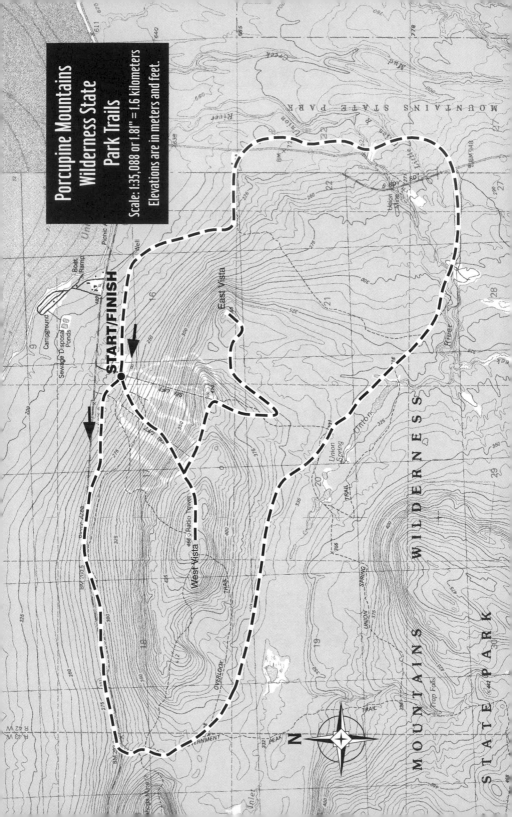

Porcupine Mountains
Wilderness State
Park Trails

Scale: 1:35,088 or 1.81" = 1.6 kilometers
Elevations are in meters and feet.

falls that will drop you from 1,400 feet to the 1,100-foot level in a big hurry on most-difficult trails like Double and Triple.

You can take Double all the way down in a sweeping arc to the most-difficult-rated Big Hemlock Trail, a great cruiser that, from here eastward, parallels the Carp River and changes its name when it meets with the Union Spring Trail. It's here that you'll encounter one of the park's warming shelters. Rest and tell tales of that harrowing just-completed descent, have lunch, wax up, or warm up.

The park's most popular route, however, is the combination of the more-difficult Nonesuch and River Trail Loops.

The Nonesuch starts off with a 2-kilometer spur that connects the lodge area to the River Trail. Head due east from the chalet, following the route of an old tram that leads to the legendary Nonesuch copper mine in the park's southeastern corner. I say "legendary" because the owners of the Nonesuch—the name itself means "exceptional"—thought it would be the most-productive copper mine in the area when it opened. It never lived up to expectations, though, and after several tries between 1866 and 1913 was finally abandoned. You won't see the mine from the trail; it's farther inland.

Then you're going the other way on River Trail, one of the park's first marked ski trails. There's a lot of varied intermediate terrain here as well as fantastic scenery. Some stretches are straight and flat so you can cover plenty of ground on crisp tracks; others allow you to reflect on the beauty around you through quiet hemlock and cedar forests. The most scenic is the 3-kilometer stretch following the Union River. There are numerous small waterfalls and rapids as the river courses through uncovered bedrock formations on its way to Lake Superior to the north. There's even a separate 2-kilometer skaters-only trail that dips down south and crosses the Little Union River before heading north. It's rated easiest. Just past the Union River Cabin—which also is available for rent for the unique experience of staying overnight with only firelight from a wood-burning stove to keep you company—you'll cross the Union River, then turn for an easy 1.5-kilo-

Directions at a glance

KILOMETER

0.0 From lodge enter Deer Yard Trail.

1.5 Turn right across snowmobile trail.

3.5 Continue through Superior Loop Trail intersection.

3.6 Continue through second Superior Loop Trail intersection.

4.1 Return to lodge.

meter section. From the next trail intersection, there's another 1.5 kilometer uphill leg ending in a twisty 100-foot drop that beginners and even low intermediates might want to think about walking down. Once you're at the bottom, you'll meet Nonesuch Loop for the trek back to the lodge.

For a different experience and a climb that'll test your lungs, head out from the lodge on Deer Yard Trail. It's only 3.75 kilometers, but it'll take you through a large, active white-tailed deer yard—an area where deer naturally gather to wait out the winter—in a majestic old-growth hemlock forest. Going out, there's a nice 100-foot drop. Superior Loop, a separate 1.75 kilometer loop for beginner skiers, merges with Deer Yard for an easy ski back. Deer Yard turns west for the remaining 2 kilometers, with skiers facing a close-to-200-foot climb that's rated most-difficult for the next-to-last leg. It's also the trail access to the Whitetail Overnight Cabin on the Lake Superior shoreline.

Superior Loop is the park's only trail that requires no ski pass. It cuts though a wispy balsam fir and birch forest and is lighted by kerosene lanterns for three hours after sunset on Saturday evening during the season.

If you're a snowshoer, you've come to the right place. 'Shoers visiting the park will want to stop at the ski chalet to learn about snow depths and possible routes. If you're headed cross-country or far into the park's interior, leave an itinerary. You can explore the deer yards along Lake Superior, the virgin hemlock forests, or the east and west overlook areas. Better yet, first-timers here may want to take advantage of the guided hikes offered by the park. They're offered during Christmas ski week— usually the week between Christmas and New Year's—and every weekend through the season.

Generally, three treks are offered. One visits an active deer yard; along the way your guide will explain just how these animals survive the winter. On Saturday night starting at sunset, 'shoe with a guide along Superior Loop to a campfire where you can thaw out a bit, sip some hot cider, and talk with the naturalist about the hemlock and birch forest you're in. The trek is free. The East Vista Hike starts with a chairlift ride to the top. You can practice on your skills as you walk over. As a bonus on this trek, both adult and children's snowshoes are available free on a first-come, first-served basis at the ski lodge. This and the trek by lantern light are perfect for never-ever 'shoers.

If you come on the last Saturday of February, you're in time for the SnowBurst Festival, including ski races, hayrides, guided snowshoe hikes, a spaghetti dinner, a torchlight parade, fireworks, and more. The Porkies is where it's at for skinny skiers and 'shoers.

Active Backwoods Retreat Trails

Active Backwoods Retreat, Ironwood

Trail type: ▬ ◄ ⬤⬤⬤

Notes: There are separate skating trails and a 5 kilometer designated snowshoe trail that winds between the cross-country trails.

Location: E-5299 West Pioneer Road, about 3 miles south of U.S. 2 in Ironwood. From U.S. 2 go south on Lake Street. Turn east onto Frenchtown Road and continue south as it curves around past Pine Street. You're now on South Range Road. Take it to the end at West Pioneer Road and the ski area.

Also used by: No one.

Distance: 33 kilometers.

Terrain: Active Backwoods Retreat features generally moderate terrain for beginning and intermediate skiers. The majority of the trail system is a heavily wooded mix of hardwoods and conifers with beautiful bluffs and old streambeds leading down into the Montreal River basin. The highest vertical climbs and drops you'll be facing are about 200 feet. Most of these are gradual—with a few notable exceptions.

Trail difficulty: Easiest to most difficult.

Surface quality: Groomed, track set, and packed for skating daily or as needed.

Food and facilities: The warming lodge has lockers available for rent, and it also has a sauna, available for $4.00 per person ($8.00 minimum). The fee includes towel and shower. There's a rustic cabin 0.4 kilometer in on the trail available for overnight or daytime rental for $30.00 per night for two and $5.00 per night for each additional person. Firewood and drinking water are supplied. Trail fees are $8.00 daily from opening through Christmas, then $5.00 daily afterward; $2.00 for children ages 8 and under. An annual family pass is $175.00. Night skiing passes cost $3.00. Loops aren't lighted. This is a real experience skiing in guided groups either by headlamp—some are available to borrow—or by moonlight. Night skiing is from 6:00. to 8:00 P.M. the first and third Tuesday of each month, and there is moonlit skiing one Saturday each month. Call to find out which one. Accommodations in the area are numerous and include lodging at a couple of downhill ski resorts, including Indianhead Mountain. The Black River Lodge has 24 rooms, an indoor pool, and more cross-country skiing trails near the Black River Scenic Byway. Numerous places to eat nearby include the

Regal Country Inn & Ice Cream Parlor for desserts, soups, and sandwiches. There's a hospital in Ironwood.

Phone numbers: Active Backwoods Retreat Trails, (906) 932–3502; Web site, www.michiweb.com/abrski. Indianhead Mountain, (906) 229–5181 or (800) 346–3426; Web site, www.indianheadmtn. com. Black River Lodge, (906) 932–3857 or (800) 666–9916. Regal Country Inn & Ice Cream Parlor, (906) 229–5122. Western U.P. Convention & Visitors Bureau, (906) 932–4850.

ERIC ANDERSON decided that his day job as an engineer at a Detroit-area auto parts company wasn't as rewarding as a life in the Upper Peninsula woods, and cross-country skiers are the better for his decision. Eric and his father, Dave, spent the last 15 years creating this gem of a ski area out of 400 acres of woodlands bordering the Montreal River, which flows north and south between Michigan and Wisconsin near this westernmost city of the Upper Peninsula.

Following natural contours, ABR—short for Active Backwoods Retreat—is one of the best reasons to head here to ski. It also has the advantage of having great lake-effect snowfalls in the early season. The result is great early conditions that stay great well into April. Up to 250 inches of snow each year is pretty normal.

An easy trail, curiously named Easy Trail, winds entirely through the property, so beginners will feel that they've actually done some skiing, not just a few simple loops with no scenery. Easy Trail generally follows an old streambed and traverses the contour lines. Tougher loops go over them. Easy Trail is one of the most popular loops in the system, because it takes you right down to the riverside. It's wide, for striding only, with a beautiful tree canopy along nearly its entire 3.5 kilometers. And it's almost all downhill to the river.

Leave the parking lot and Easy Trail breaks to your left from the more-difficult-rated River Trail. Intermediate skiers can take River Trail and meet later with their beginner friends, because the two intersect in a few spots along the way. On the way Easy Trail striders will go by some 150-year-old white pines that were passed up in the 1850s,

Directions at a glance

KILOMETER

0.0 Leave from trailhead on East Trail/River Trail.

0.1 Continue on Easy Trail.

1.0 Rejoin River Trail.

1.8 Easy Trail veers left.

2.4 Continue on Easy Trail.

2.9 Go through intersection on Easy Trail.

3.5 Return to start.

Active Backwoods Retreat Trails
Scale: 1:9,645 or 6.6" = 1.6 kilometers

START/
FINISH 1552

Gravel Pit

*1491

CHICAGO

1488

1500

Gravel Pits

1600

04

2

Montreal

GOGEBIC CO.

AND IRON CO.

1500

1500

1500

35

1530

N

On the trail at Active Backwoods Retreat.

when this area was logged virtually to bare ground. East flattens out as it approaches its first intersection with River Trail. They join up for a few kilos, then Easy breaks off to your right as it heads straight down to the river at a spot called the Swimming Hole.

Beginners can extend their treks at this point, but check your energy levels. If you want to be out for more than an hour or so, turn right onto the easiest-rated Jack Pine Trail. It follows the river for quite a way on a flat floodplain through a pine plantation that offers another great canopy and protection from any weather.

The trail here is two-way and double track set, so you won't have any problems meeting skiers coming the other way. In fact, it's a great place to stop and chat with your fellow striders. Be sure to watch for a special treat on one of the bends: On the Wisconsin side of the river is a unique round barn made of stone. You can take a couple of side loops that go around the base of a hill here, or simply turn around and head back to the intersection.

Easy and River Trails then follow the river southward. At the inter-section known as High Rock, Easy veers left off through the start of an old sand pit. Through a stand of hemlock, you'll start a slow, gradual climb. There are a few stubby hills you might have to herringbone up, but if you have the right ski bottoms or wax, you can push through them if you stay on the tracks. Past this gradual slope you'll be back in the other side of the streambed you began on, just before the intersection with Sunset Trail, rated more difficult. Here you might be entering the prettiest sections of the entire system, a cedar swamp. Because it's a wetland, the Andersons built a wooden boardwalk through the entire area. Easy brushes with River Trail again, then the two separate. Easy Trail, still in that swamp area, heads across a flat section along the northern side of Blueberry Bluff, a neat rock formation that forms a 70-foot sheer cliff with quite a few ice formations hanging off—hence its nickname, the Ice Falls. You'll then sail through a block of oak and white pine back to the starter oval loop and the parking lot.

If you're looking for a great, short intermediate loop, try that 2.5-kilometer Sunset Trail. It's the oldest in the system and available for striding only. It's short and somewhat hilly. Start off on River Trail this time, heading up and down some short hills and through intermittent clearings in the woods. A bit past the rustic trailside cabin and a pit toilet, Sunset turns left, bouncing over some nice, moderate hills before looping eastward to join up with the 5.5-kilometer River Trail.

River is the most popular more difficult loop. Leave the parking lot and, once you're past the Sunset Trail cutoff, the fun begins. You'll make a nice, gradual climb of about 70 feet onto a ridge. Up on top you'll have a beautiful stand of Norway pine on your left, while off to the east you'll see the parking lot, trailhead, and forest beyond. You'll climb maybe another 20 to 30 feet before heading into a downhill run featuring about a 100-foot drop into a great stand of maple. These are very doable hills with no sharp curves. You can either snowplow or coast to the next option, open only to advanced skiers. Once you get there, you'll see why.

The 1.4-kilometer Popple Plunge is aptly named. You're at the edge of a trail that drops nearly straight off the table for about 150 feet into an aspen grove. Beginners or true intermediates will want to stick to the trail to your left, which bypasses all this. If you elect and survive the Plunge, the trail goes through some nice rollers through that same aspen grove. You'll be going downhill virtually all the way until the trail curves left, where you'll lose your speed. Then you've got to climb back up 150 feet through a series of loops to the elevation you left, to rejoin River Trail. If you're not hardcore, stick with River Trail, which meets with the bottom side of Popple Plunge perhaps 100 yards from its start.

The second major hill on River Trail is up next. You'll drop about 100 feet on a nice, gradual, fun hill that drifts slightly right before meeting with Easy Trail. Either follow Easy for the shorter, gentle coast down to the Montreal River or take the longer track on River, which loops through the old sand pit for a bit before heading to the river. There's another advanced option here: Pit Point Trail. River Trail then heads south along the Montreal until a point known as High Rock, where you'll climb about 100 feet, descend eastward down a 60-foot hill, then climb another short but very steep hill just before the intersection with Sulo's Loop. It might be the toughest climb on the entire system, hard for even the groomers to tackle. You can add another 3.8 kilometers by taking this easiest-rated loop through an old open marsh.

Avoid Sulo's by heading left at the intersection and continuing on River Trail around Bard's Bump—which also can be avoided through a shortcut. Bard's is relatively open and you'll be climbing up and down old dunes. Past it you'll brush up against Easy Trail in the sand pit again, then you're in for another long, gradual 80-foot hoof uphill to Blueberry Bluff. The Ice Falls will be below you. You'll head through a heavy stand of red oak. From here you'll have one last downhill, a nice 100-foot drop that, if you maintain enough speed, will let you coast across a field nearly back to the parking lot.

Active Backwoods Retreat is a great little find and one you'll want to keep coming back to for a taste of that great Upper Peninsula scenery.

West Michigan

While most skiers head north to the forested areas of West Michigan from Grand Rapids northward, there are pockets of greatness, albeit on the small side, below the snowbelt, too, with great conditions, great trails, and great snow. I'll highlight a few areas in the south, but if you want the best conditions, the best snow, and the most consistent scenery, go north, young skier. After a short tour, I will too.

Kalamazoo Nature Center Trails

Kalamazoo Nature Center, Kalamazoo

Trail type: ▬▬▬

Note: No off-trail travel permitted except in the 11-acre arboretum.

Location: 700 North Westnedge Avenue, about 12 minutes north of downtown Kalamazoo. From I–94, take U.S. 131 north and exit 41 east. Follow Business Loop 131 to North Westnedge, and head north to the center on your right.

Also used by: The occasional hiker.

Distance: 11 trails totaling 8 miles.

Terrain: Gently rolling terrain through magnificent stands of mostly virgin beech and maple forest encompassing 1,000 acres.

Trail dificulty: Easiest to more difficult. River Vista Trail is not recommended for skiers.

Surface quality: Ungroomed, but there is usually a skier-set track. Call ahead for trail conditions, since snow quality and quantity can vary.

Food and facilities: The nature center features an indoor teaching facility with lots of exhibits for children focusing on the fauna and flora of south-central Lower Michigan. Trails are open during the center's hours, 9:00 A.M. to 5:00 P.M. Monday through Saturday, 1:00 to 5:00 P.M. Sunday. Gates close at 6:00 P.M. Closed Thanksgiving, January 1, December 24 and 25. Admission is $4.50 for adults, $3.50 for ages 55 and older, $2.50 for ages 4–13; children under 3 are free. No ski rentals on site. Lodging choices include the beautifully restored Stuart Avenue Inn Bed and Breakfast and the Radisson Plaza Hotel at Kalamazoo Center, with 281 rooms, a health club, and a pool, attached to a downtown shopping mall. There's a hospital in Kalamazoo.

Phone numbers: Kalamazoo Nature Center, (616) 381–1574; Web site, www.naturecenter.org. Stuart Avenue Inn, (616) 342–0230. Radisson Plaza Hotel at Kalamazoo Center, (616) 343–3333. For other choices including ski rental locations, contact the Kalamazoo Convention and Visitors Bureau, (616) 381–4003; Web site, www.kazoofun.com.

LOCATED ON THE OUTSKIRTS of one of Michigan's largest cities, the 1,100-acre nature center's summer hiking trails serve double duty in winter for cross-country skiers. Due to variable snow conditions, it's wise to call

Kalamazoo Nature Center's Delano Homestead.

ahead before planning your trip. On Monday when your friends are brag-
ging around the copier about how many miles they chalked up, these routes
may not sound like much, but they make up for it in beauty, history, and a
wilderness setting so close to one of Michigan's major southern cities.

Most trails leave from the Interpretive Center. Each is short, but if
you combine several, you'll have a good workout. Head to your left onto
Habitat Haven, a pretty 0.6-mile route that traverses a beech-maple forest and a swamp, and overlooks a pond and part of Trout Run Stream
(don't expect to see trout, though, because it's slow moving and may be
frozen). Take off your skis to negotiate the steps where it joins up with
Beech-Maple Trail at the eastern end. It connects with the more-difficult
but short 0.2-mile-long Cooper's Overlook. If you're starting at the Interpretive Center, you've got to take Beech-Maple Trail to get to Cooper's.
The most enjoyable way to ski it would be to start from Habitat Haven.
Where it meets Cooper's, take off your skis, climb the short flight of
stairs, and start a gradual downhill run on a beautiful ridge that's covered
with hardwoods looking out over Trout Run Stream and festooned with
large trailside logs. The trail is named for the glen, which is in turn named
for 19th-century author James Fenimore Cooper, who visited relatives in
the area and spent time in the glen. Cooper compiled information on pioneer life to use in his book *Oak Openings*, named for the natural clearings

in which families built their homes. The glen and overlook harbor spectacular stands of beech and maple.

Pioneer Woods is the nature center's longest at 1.7 miles, and one of its most varied as well. It's rated more difficult. Reach it across Westnedge from the Interpretive Center. It starts at the parking lot for the Delano Farm Homestead (yes, a distant relative of President Franklin Delano Roosevelt) and glides into or near many of the oak openings dotting the landscape here. From the lot head pretty much due south along the forest windbreaks adjacent to the demonstration croplands at the restored 1858 farmstead.

The trail then loops through a spectacular old-growth beech-maple forest where you can either turn right for a quick trip back to the homestead, or go left to travel an out-and-back trail through the woods to Source Pond, where Trout Run Stream starts. Double back from the pond and you've got two choices: Either take the same route, or head through the woods on the 0.6-mile Trout Run Trail, also rated more difficult. It borders the stream before curling back to rejoin Pioneer Woods. Because of the heavy-duty climb up to it—anywhere from 100 to 200 feet—River Vista Trail isn't recommended for skiers. Beech-Maple Trail is a mostly more-difficult run that begins at the common trailhead for Habitat Haven and Valley. It's a 0.6-mile trek rated most difficult because of a 30-foot climb or descent about midway, depending on which way you go.

Beech-Maple, named for the beautiful stand of trees it pushes through, runs south then wiggles along the northern side of Trout Run Stream, where there's an overlook. Just before the railroad tracks, it makes a hairpin turn left for that 30-foot climb and returns to the

Directions at a glance

MILE

0.0   From Delano Homestead lot head south.

0.5   Veer right to follow loop.

0.8   Turn left (for longer trek, turn right).

1.0   Veer left through intersections back to starting trail.

1.6   Return to lot.

trailhead area. The nature center itself is considered one of the state's best. Newly renovated, it has lots of hands-on exhibits for your kids. There's a butterfly house and a wildlife viewing room where visitors watch and hear feeding birds through outdoor microphones.

This great set of shorter trails will, if you're a Cooper fan, perhaps take you on a trip into the mind of the writer, watching him gather story material and memories here that he incorporated into some of the greatest American romantic novels of all time. And you'll have a great ski, too.

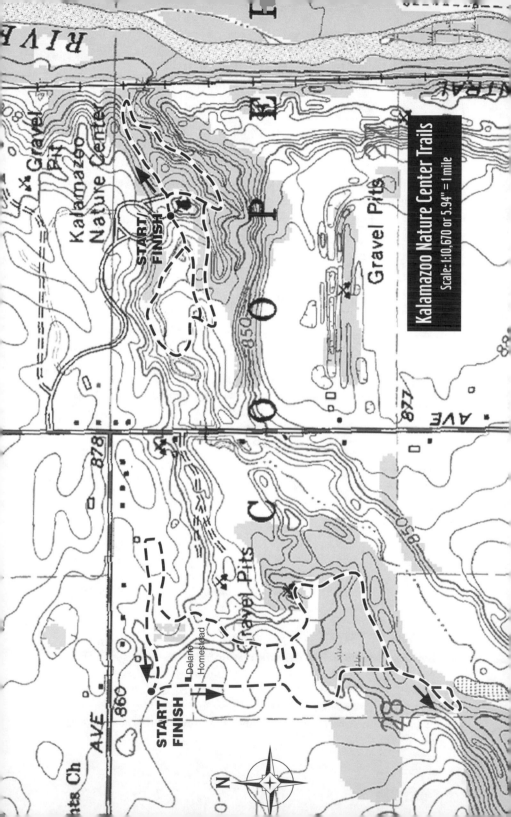

Kalamazoo Nature Center Trails

Scale: 1:10,670 or 5.94" = 1 mile

START/FINISH

START/FINISH

Kalamazoo Nature Center

Gravel Pit

Gravel Pits

Gravel Pits

Delano Homestead

RIVER

AVE

AVE

N

Yankee Springs State Recreation Area Trails

Yankee Springs State Recreation Area, Middleville

Trail type: ▬▬▬

Location: 2104 Gun Lake Road, Middleville. From U.S. 131 take exit 61. Go east on Road A-42 for about 8 miles to the park entrance.

Also used by: Trails are traversed by snowmobile routes in several spots.

Distance: About 7 miles over six loops.

Terrain: Trails traverse mostly hilly land in this part of West Michigan, with a few steeps to make things interesting; climbs range up to 30 feet.

Trail dificulty: Easiest to most difficult. Trails are omnidirectional.

Surface quality: Groomed and single track set.

Food and facilities: A ski lodge, open weekends, with a fireplace and pit toilets is near the Long Lake Outdoor Center, just north of Gun Lake Road. The park also has several rustic trailside cabins available for rent throughout the year. You must bring your own sleeping bags. More information is available through the park office. Accommodations nearby include Hastings' Parkview Motel, a basic place with 18 rooms. Still more places to stay are in Grand Rapids to the north and Kalamazoo to the south. There are lots of places to eat along U.S. 131 to the west of the park, in the Middleville area, in Kalamazoo to the south, and north near Grand Rapids. Hospitals are found in Hastings, Grand Rapids, and Kalamazoo.

Phone numbers: Yankee Springs State Recreation Area, (616) 795–9081. Hastings' Parkview Motel, (616) 945–9511. Barry County Area Chamber of Commerce, (616) 945–2454. Grand Rapids/Kent County Convention and Visitors Bureau, (616) 459–8287 or (800) 678–9859; Web site, www.grcvb.org. Kalamazoo County Convention and Visitors Bureau, (616) 381–4003; Web site, www.kzoofun.com.

THE HILLS OF SOUTHWESTERN Lower Michigan harbor some surprisingly good cross-country skiing, and this recreation area—the state's euphemism for spots that offer more recreation opportunities than do state parks—is one of the best places to find them. Hugging the northern shoreline of Gun Lake, one of the area's largest and best, this 5,000-acre facility was once a Native American hunting ground, the home of the famous Chief Noonday.

It was also the site of Yankee Springs, a village established in 1835 by Yankee Bill Lewis, who ran a stagecoach stop here on the route between Kalamazoo and Grand Rapids. There are still lots of deer, grouse, and other wildlife to be encountered on the trails, most of which you'll find in the area of Long and Hall Lakes, in the park's center. The recreation area's trail map designates all the routes most difficult. The explanation is that anytime there's a significant hill on a route, the entire route gets that rating. However, there are some gentler passes available, too.

The park's most popular cross-country ski trails leave from the warming lodge off Gun Lake Road near the Long Lake Outdoor Center. There's a gentle 0.4-mile run that many take. It circles the lodge and is great for beginners. It's pretty flat, except for two fairly gentle 40-foot downhill slopes that are spread over about

Trails cut through thick stands of woods at Yankee Springs.

100 yards each. The route drops down to its westernmost point near the shore of Long Lake, one of nine in the complex. It's not that far of a drop for intermediates, but it's a challenge for first-timers. There's a similar climb back up toward the lodge.

Advanced skiers may want to tackle the loop just west of Hall Lake. It's probably the hilliest of all loops in the winter sports area. From the lodge head about 0.2 mile southwest from marker A to I, the Hall Lake trailhead. Turn right then make a sharp left, which will take you over some small hills through a pine forest. You're traveling east now toward the lake on a slight downhill run.

As you near the lake, the trail flattens out. You'll turn left and run along the lakeshore then begin to climb, and as you turn away from the water, you'll discover what all that climbing was about when you encounter your first big uphill, a quick rise of about 30 feet, followed by a sharp right-hander at the top. Except for a brief drop into a gully, you'll be climbing again shortly as you head away from the water toward marker H. Another downhill awaits between markers H and J, along

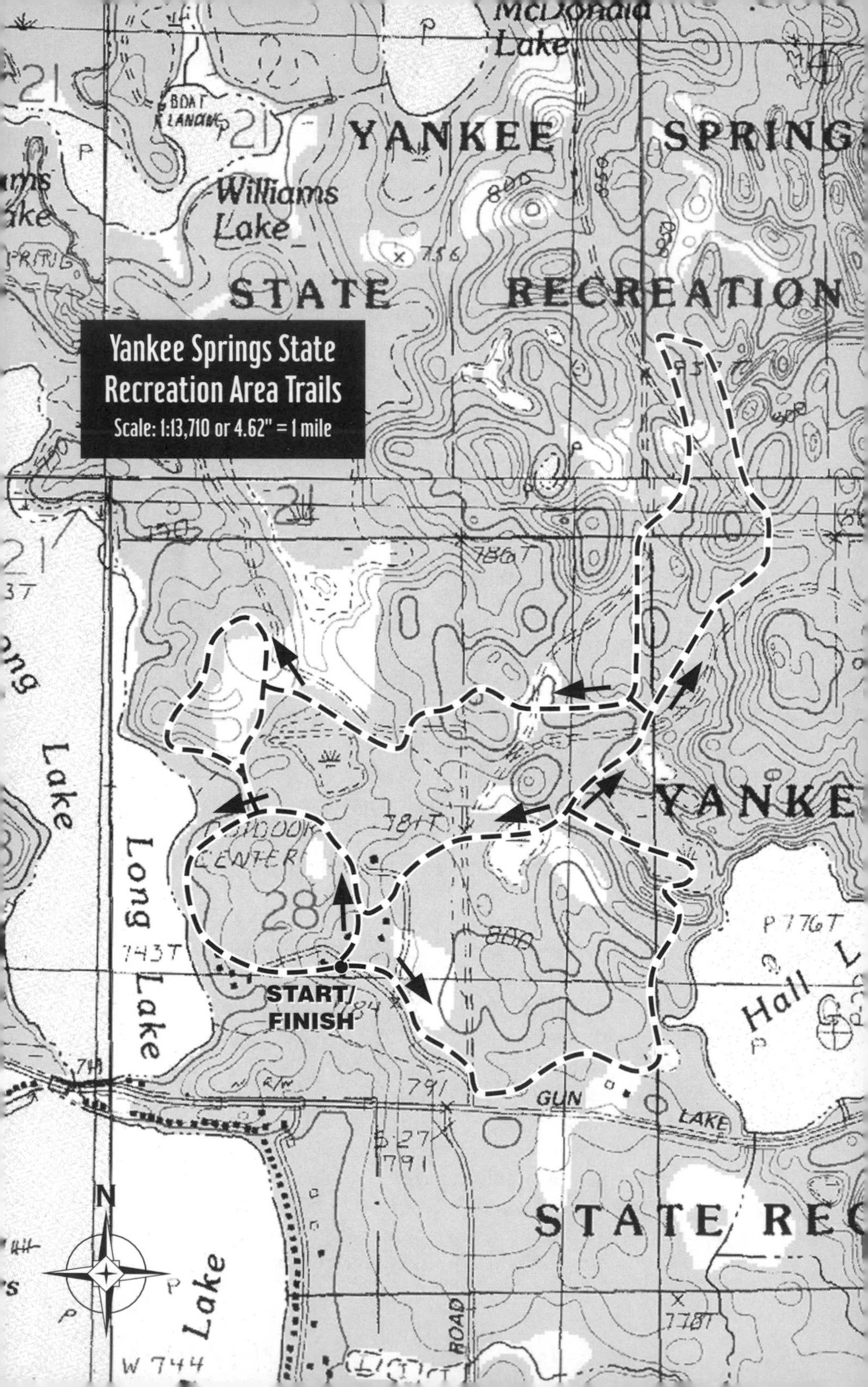

Yankee Springs State Recreation Area Trails
Scale: 1:13,710 or 4.62" = 1 mile

YANKEE SPRING

STATE RECREATION

YANKE

YANKEE SPRING

McDonald Lake

Williams Lake

BOAT LANDING

Long Lake

OUTDOOR CENTER

START/FINISH

Hall L

Gun Lake

STATE REC

N

with a sharp drop of 30 feet. At J turn left toward marker I and up another grade. This segment is particularly tricky, because just before that rise of about 30 feet, the trail is narrow. From here the trail goes left, straightens out through an open area, and heads back to the start. You can avoid that last hill by taking a 0.2-mile jaunt back from J to A toward the lodge if you go straight rather than turning left. Or go the opposite direction to take advantage of the downhill segments to give yourself a respite from the climbs.

You can extend your trip by about a mile by turning right at marker H and heading past Grave's Hill, one of the highest points in the recreation area. Continue northward through the groves of pines and along a power line to climb, then sail up another hill of about 30 feet as you track north toward marker F. You'll also pass the area known as the Devil's Soupbowl, a large valley formed when glaciers scoured the earth here, leaving the gravel deposits that form the hills around you. You won't be able to see it, however.

Directions at a glance

MILE

0.0   Leave warming lodge.

0.2   Turn left at I.

1.1   Turn left at H.

1.2   Turn left at J.

1.6   Turn right at I.

1.9   Return to warming lodge.

At F you can turn left and backtrack 0.6 mile along a power line to marker E, where you can turn left and, a few strides later, find yourself back at marker G for the run back. If you choose to go right at E on your way back to the warming lodge, get ready for two last hills—first a downhill, then an uphill—in the 0.2-mile trip over to marker L, in the midst of a pine plantation. The hill near marker E is spread out over a longer section. There's a shorter climb approaching L. The 0.4 mile between markers L and C, then left past marker D within sight of Long Lake, is more difficult ground. Turn right at B again to make the easiest-rated loop close to the lake, which brings you back to the warming lodge. This ski from marker E will have taken you on another 1.3 miles.

Yankee Springs is a great example of a great oasis of nature in a sea of fast-encroaching urban development. We're indeed lucky it has been preserved forever.

Pigeon Creek Park Trails
Pigeon Creek Park, Grand Haven

Trail type: ➤ ➤ ◄ ⬤

Location: 14 Washington Street, Grand Haven. The entrance is on Stanton Road, 3 miles east of U.S. 31. The area is in a 415-acre park operated by Ottawa County.

Also used by: Occasional hikers. There's a sledding hill on site, but away from ski trails.

Distance: 16 kilometers spread over 15 loops.

Terrain: Set in wooded dunes approximately 6 miles from the Lake Michigan shoreline. There are elevation changes of up to 60 feet.

Trail dificulty: Easiest to most difficult.

Surface quality: Groomed regularly. Single track set with trails for striding and skating.

Food and facilities: There's a large warming lodge with food and refreshments. Trail use is free. Ski rentals are available for youths and adults, and skating skis are available at the lodge. Rentals run $6.00 for two hours and $2.00 per hour thereafter. Youths, $4.00 for two hours, and $2.00 after that. Skating skis run $8.00 for two hours, $2.00 per hour thereafter (1999 rates). Snowshoe rentals are $6.00 for two hours, $3.00 per hour thereafter. Rentals are also available at Breakaway Bicycles in Grand Haven and other locations in Holland and Cascade. Accommodations and restaurants are available in Grand Haven. Accommodations include the Days Inn, with 100 rooms and an indoor pool. Restaurants include the Stable Inn south of Grand Haven along U.S. 31. There's a hospital in Grand Haven. More information on the area is available from the Grand Haven/Spring Lake Area Visitors Bureau.

Phone numbers: Pigeon Creek Park conditions, (231) 738–9531. Breakaway Bicycles, (231) 844–1199. Days Inn, (231) 842–1999. Stable Inn, (231) 846–8581. Grand Haven/Spring Lake Area Visitors Bureau, (800) 303–4097.

JUST OUTSIDE ONE of the West Michigan coastline's most charming towns is one of the finest areas open for public use in southwestern Lower Michigan. The majority of runs are intended for families, ranging from beginner to more difficult, with a few toughies thrown in for good measure and even two lighted trails. (Trails are lighted nightly when conditions permit.) The trails are far enough from shore that the area is a prime candidate for huge lake-effect snowfalls.

In most areas you'd pay to ski trails like these, but here the county funds them and use is free. Once you've reracked your skis, break out the sleds for a couple of runs down the lighted hill located along one of the ridgelines near the Pigeon Creek Lodge. You must bring your own, however.

From the lodge the most popular loop combo is to head out on Berghorst Trail, rated easiest, and link up with North Berghorst, another easiest-rated, tracked loop. Take off on North Berghorst and striders or skaters can turn left for the full tour onto intermediate-rated Sugar Maple Lane, which gradually loops counterclockwise to the south. Where Sugar Maple jogs hard left, you'll cross the North Berghorst skating loop again.

If you can handle it, continue straight on to South Berghorst. This 0.6-kilometer section is rated most difficult because of the quick 50-foot drop onto the floodplain of Pigeon Creek. It's a nice straight plunge with no turns until you're at the bottom, well past the ridge. Once you're down turn left, crossing two bridges over a couple of small creeks. After the second bridge kick off your skis if you wish and walk out to Creek View, an overlook of the valley. Then veer off to your left onto the more-difficult striding trail that bears along the ridge overlooking Pigeon Creek, or continue down, then up the floodplain faces on most-difficult-rated and ungroomed Hemlock Path. You'll be first dropping down, then climbing up a fairly steep 40-foot ridge on Hemlock. It meets up with that intermediate path about 0.6 kilometer later.

Pigeon Creek facilities include a large lodge, where trails begin.

From there either continue back to the lodge on the bailout route, an easiest-rated 0.4-kilometer trek atop the ridge, or go straight to find yourself on a flat run—that is, until you turn right. When you do, you're on Pigeon Plunge, a very steep 60-foot dive with a more gradual runout into easiest-rated trails back to the lodge, straight ahead another 0.9 kilometer. Pigeon Plunge is about all most folks who don't ski anywhere but the Midwest will want to face.

Cross Stanton Street to the park's northern side and you'll find the going a lot flatter, with hills of no more than 20 feet. The main Northside Trail Loop is more than 3 kilometers and is a nice, nearly flat easiest run, but intermediates will be happy they jutted off to your right onto Mounds Loop. You'll be in the narrow confines of a dense jack pine forest, with lots of undulating loops for the beginning and end portions of your 1.6 kilometer tour before you rejoin Northside Trail. Inside Northside is Old Corral, a flat, easiest-rated 1.6-kilometer tracked loop.

At night follow the trail markers on the map. Both skaters and striders can enjoy this route. Trail 1 leads south from the lodge past the sledding hill; 10 heads east, and 11 goes north to bring you back to the lodge. The newest 1.3-kilometer lighted trail will take you in a large rectangle from the lodge west along Berghorst, south through some fairly flat terrain with a few small rolling hills, then back to the east before the northern leg leads you back to the lodge. The routes are softly lighted, still dark enough to see the stars, an experience best enjoyed with a close companion.

Directions at a glance

KILOMETER

0.0   From lodge head onto Berghorst.

0.3   Turn left at intersection.

0.6   Turn left at intersection.

0.9   Turn left at intersection.

1.3   Return to lodge.

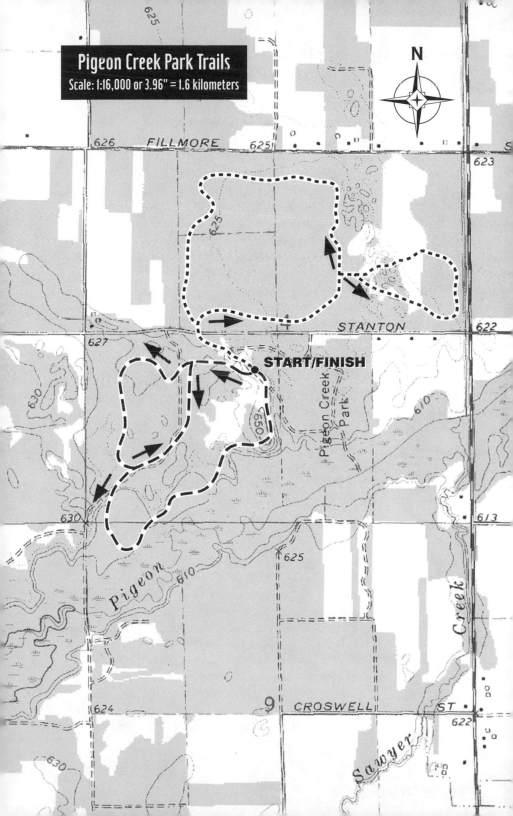

Muskegon State Park Trails

Muskegon State Park, North Muskegon

Trail type: ═══ ◄ ▦

Note: A lighted trail has both a single track set and skating lanes. There are snowshoe trails of 2 kilometers and 5 kilometers. The trail map identifies different routes by numbers at each intersection.

Location: In Muskegon State Park, 3560 Memorial Drive, North Muskegon. The actual ski park is located on Scenic Drive. From U.S. 31 follow the signs for Muskegon State Park. Take the North Muskegon exit and go up Whitehall Road to Giles Road. Take Giles west until it ends. Turn south onto Scenic Drive and follow it to the park.

Distance: 8 kilometers total, including about 7 kilometers of brightly lighted trails, which are open nightly.

Terrain: A slightly rolling to nearly flat sand dune area, except for some steeper stabilized dunes. The 2.5-kilometer beginner loop has one small, gentle hill. The 5-kilometer intermediate loop also has a hill that can be bypassed, with heights of more than 300 feet. Most of the trails leave from the vicinity of the lodge.

Trail dificulty: Easiest to most difficult.

Surface quality: Groomed daily, single track set. Trails are omnidirectional.

Food and facilities: There is a park entry permit fee of $4.00 daily or $20.00 annually per car. Trail fees are $4.00 for adults; children under 12 and seniors 65 and over pay $2.00 daily Monday through Friday. On weekends it's $5.00 for adults and $3.00 for kids and seniors. Season passes are available. Ski and snowshoe rentals are available at the park sports lodge: $6.00 for the first two hours, $7.00 for skating skis. The lodge has soda pop, hot drinks, and some snacks and is open daily 10:00 A.M. to 7:00 P.M. Pit toilets are available on the trail, weather permitting. Accommodations in the area include the Comfort Inn, with 117 rooms and an indoor pool. Places to eat include the Doo Drop Inn in Muskegon for good family fare. There are many others in the area. More information on the Muskegon area is available from the Muskegon County Convention and Visitors Bureau. There's a hospital in Muskegon.

Phone numbers: Muskegon State Park, (231) 744–3480. Comfort Inn, (231) 739–9092. Doo Drop Inn, (231) 755–3791. Muskegon County Convention and Visitors Bureau, (231) 722–3751; Web site, www.visitmuskegon.org.

THE COMMUNITY that once was known as the Queen City for its lumber which helped build America's West in the 19th century, is now known, among other things, as the location of one of the nation's only luge runs, within this 1,350-acre park on the northern side of Muskegon Lake. The park's dunes hold numerous hiking trails, some of which double as a cross-country ski range. As a result of the big dunes that have been piled up behind the beaches, some of the ski trails are fairly rugged. All trails are designated by numbered intersection markers.

Those preferring an easy trip are advised to stick to the 2.5-kilometer easiest loop. Start out at the northern end from the lodge (where most of the trails leave from). Beginners should follow the trail loops starting with marker 5. It's a nice run around the northern end of the luge run, then eastern through the woods through a series of ess turns to marker 6. Here beginners can head out to your left toward marker 7, then turn right at 8 for a straight run through the intersection at marker 4 and back to 5 and the lodge. This route parallels part of the park's lighted trail segment.

Most folks with their ski legs, however, will want to continue on a basic more-difficult loop that traverses most of the trail system on a nice zigzag route through the park. Start off on the easiest run from marker 5 to the intersection that takes you to 6. Instead of heading left, go right to marker 4. The trail then makes several ess turns to get to marker 3. Keep going straight to 9, then straight again to marker 10. Go straight through the intersection and the trail will take first a short loop to the right, then a fairly sharp turn to the left before a run up a gradual hill to marker 12 right along the park boundary, near Lost Lake, which you'll be able to see through the woods. Turn left here for a short trip to marker 11, then head due west over some nice, rolling more-difficult terrain on another

Zoom down a tree-covered dune at Muskegon State Park.

arrow-straight run to marker 10. Turn right back to 9, then right again back up to marker 8, and finish by taking a left turn for the long, lazy run back to marker 4, marker 5, and the lodge. Most of this run is also on the lighted trail.

Advanced skiers might want to take the trail out to marker 9, then turn toward the lake. You'll be making a short, steep climb of close to 200 feet between markers 9 and 2, and another 100 more if you turn left at 2 and head to marker 1. You'll lose most of that altitude between markers 1 and 10. Another trail, the Spencer Weersing Memorial Trail, named for a local ski enthusiast, is rated most difficult. It's a squiggly little route that climbs 85 feet with great overlooks of Scenic Drive before turning back to marker 2. Be ready for two great downhills with sharp turns, especially once you start heading off the overlook. The 85-foot drops take in two hills, with a hairpin left-hander at the bottom. You'll be traveling mostly over wooded dune country here.

> ## Directions at a glance
>
> KILOMETER
>
> 0.0 Leave from left at sports lodge.
>
> 2.5 Turn right at marker 6.
>
> 3.0 Turn left at marker 4.
>
> 5.0 End at rest rooms.

Snowshoers can head anywhere in the park. A great run is to parallel Scenic Drive for beautiful views of the Lake Michigan beachfront and some of the other hiking trails not generally open to skiing. For those who'd rather follow a marked route, there will soon be a designated snowshoe trail leading away from the sports complex. Check at the lodge for the route.

Muskegon State Park Trails
Scale: 1:10,000 or 6.34" = 1.6 kilometers
Elevations are in meters.

START/FINISH

CAMPGROUND

MUSKEGON

STATE PARK

BOUNDARY

SHORELINE

N

Mackenzie Cross-Country Ski Trail
Manistee National Forest, Cadillac

Trail type: ▬▬▬

Note: Omnidirectional.

Location: Within the Manistee National Forest west of Cadillac and adjacent to Caberfae Peaks downhill ski area. From Cadillac head west on MI 55 for 12 miles to Caberfae Road. Go north for 2 miles. A trail entrance is located west on 38 Road, or at the base of the Caberfae Peaks instruction hill.

Also used by: No one.

Distance: Over 9 miles of loops of varying lengths, from 0.9 mile up.

Terrain: Heavily forested glacial hills of varying heights up to 75 feet, though most are not heart-stoppers if you're used to advanced areas. Some trails are narrower than others. Overall, the area is not conducive to skating.

Trail dificulty: Easiest to most difficult.

Surface quality: Double track set for traditional skiing. Groomed regularly by volunteers.

Food and facilities: There's a parking area off 38 Road. Otherwise it might be wise to enter through Caberfae Peaks ski area, which has a new day lodge in which to warm up. Ski rentals there are $12.00 daily, and children's sizes are available. You'll find a restaurant and cafeteria on the premises, too, along with lodging. Accommodations are extensive in Cadillac, including Best Western Bill Oliver's along MI 55, which is not connected with the ski area. It features 66 rooms, an indoor pool and whirlpool, and a restaurant just west of town. Other restaurants are found along MI 55 near the motel, and in downtown Cadillac at the eastern end of Lake Cadillac. There's a hospital in Cadillac.

Phone numbers: Caberfae Peaks ski area, (231) 862–3000 or (800) YOU–SKII. Best Western Bill Oliver's, (231) 775–2458. Huron-Manistee National Forest Cadillac Headquarters, (231) 774–2421. Cadillac Convention and Visitors Bureau, (231) 775–0657 or (800) 225–2537.

SET IN THE BEAUTIFUL, rolling, hardwood hills of West Michigan, Mackenzie Trail is nearest to both downhill runs and one of northern Michigan's major resort towns. Many of the trees in the area are old growth, planted by the Civilian Conservation Corps during the depression to replenish northern Michigan's forests, which had been cut bare in the 19th-century lumber

Mackenzie Cross-Country Ski Trail
Scale: 1:20,000 or 3.12" = 1 mile
Elevations are in meters.

START/FINISH

boom. You'll be cruising through stands of beech, basswood, and maple sprinkled with evergreens, including arrow-straight CCC tree plantations.

For convenience' sake, pick up any rental skis you need at Caberfae and enter the trails from the comfort of the downhill ski area. Park in the ski area's lot, find the trailhead at the base of the runs, and head off. All trails and intersections are marked by numbers instead of names.

Here's one nice, mostly intermediate route: From Caberfae, you'll find yourself immediately on a section that starts as a flat, easiest-rated straightaway romp. At marker 21 it turns a wee bit more difficult. The trail climbs gently to cross a bridge over a small ravine, one of several on the system. Continue straight to marker 20, then make a right for 0.3 mile up a fairly gentle slope to marker 4, a section that's rated easiest. From 4 you've got a couple of choices: Either head straight and continue on the easiest system, or turn left onto the system's most-difficult portions. You'll be climbing a fairly gentle 75 feet over 1.6 miles. You should be comfortable on your skis to handle this section, but the views are worth it. You'll be traveling alongside a ravine about 75 feet deep, with beautiful views of forested hills almost as far as you can see off to the west. This section is the most difficult of the entire system. If the hills got your blood pumping a bit too much, head off to your right at marker 5 to a more-difficult trail that dips down to and then runs alongside Johnson Creek to the south for about 1.7 miles to marker 6.

Directions at a glance

MILE

0.0 From Caberfae parking lot head west.

0.6 Turn left at intersection.

0.9 Turn left at intersection.

1.5 Veer left at intersection.

3.2 Veer left at marker 6.

3.2 Veer left at marker 12.

4.0 Go through intersection at marker 13.

4.9 Turn left at marker 19.

5.0 Turn right at marker 20.

5.6 Return to lot at Caberfae.

From here on you're back into easiest-trail country. You can return in two ways: either straight or to the left to connect with an inner loop that—via markers 12, 13, 19, and back to 20—will return you to Caberfae in about 2 miles; or straight from marker 6, through 7, 8, 9, 17, 18, and 19, then back to 20 for the run back to Caberfae for a glide of about 3 miles, all on trails with an easiest rating.

If you're headed out from the 38 Road access, you'll be starting at marker 1 on an easiest section in a good 0.8-mile warm-up loop before turning right at marker 3 and heading for the rest of the system.

Cool's Cross-Country Farm Trails

Cool's Cross-Country Farm, Reed City

Trail type: ▬▬▶

Note: Skijoring also is allowed with trained dogs. All trails are two-way.

Location: 16557 210th Avenue, LeRoy, north of Reed City off U.S. 131. From U.S. 131 take exit 162. Turn west in 0.1 mile to 210th Avenue. Go north 2.5 miles to the farm.

Also used by: No one. This facility is on private property.

Distance: 25 kilometers of trails, single and double tracked.

Terrain: Trails are cut through a lush tree farm featuring several dozen varieties of trees. Climb to the top of Bald Mountain and you'll be about 300 feet higher than the lodge, and only 200 feet lower than Lower Michigan's highest elevation.

Trail dificulty: Easiest to most difficult.

Surface quality: Groomed as needed, at least weekly. Trails are groomed with a draft horse.

Food and facilities: Cool's Farm is one of the most complete cross-country ski lodges in the state. It features a restaurant and lounge at the main lodge serving sandwiches, soups, and chili as well as breakfast. There are also lots of other activities that keep people coming back, including horse-drawn rides by appointment, lodging packages, and guided tours by appointment. There is a health room with exercise equipment if you need more; wood-fired sauna and massage are available by appointment. There is also a dorm room and bunkhouses for group lodging as well as private rooms and four trailside cabins for rent, three with cooking facilities. Four unheated huts are maintained along the trails; here you can either observe the wildlife in the area or just rest. On full-moon nights Cool's offers Moon Lit Tours once a month. See the Web site for dates and times. The trails are open daily 9:00 A.M. to dark. Ski rentals are $10.00 a day or $7.00 for two hours; for children ages 12 and under, $6.00 daily and $4.00 for two hours. Trail fees run $7.50 daily, $5.50 for two hours and the moonlight skis; for children, $4.00 daily and $3.00 for two hours. Lodging fees are $30.00 per person per night, including skiing. Cabins with cooking facilities are $35.00 per person per night, and the fee also includes a ski pass. The Cools will transport your equipment to your cabin. There are hospitals in Reed City and Cadillac.

More accommodations and restaurants are available north along U.S. 131 in Cadillac and south near Reed City.

Phone numbers: Cool's Cross-Country Farm, (231) 768–4624 or (888) 225–1616; Web site, www.coolxcfarm.com.

COOL'S CROSS-COUNTRY FARM has been a family enterprise for more than 20 years and is one of the few true destination cross-country-only resorts in Michigan. Begun by Mike Cool, the operation is now carried on by his sons, who also run the 400-acre property as a tree farm. Cool's main lodge, in fact, was built from more than 16 varieties of wood grown on the property.

You may think the ski area is a bit too far south for great conditions, but in reality temperatures here average 5 degrees cooler than along the Lake Michigan lakeshore, and the area is at the southern edge of a West Michigan snowbelt. Even when there's no snow a few miles away, then, there will be snow on the trails here if the folks at Cool's tell you there is. They pride themselves on an honest review of conditions.

A trip here is not only relaxing with plenty of exercise, but educational, too, because of the many informative markers corresponding to points of interest along the trails.

Now let's look at those trails. There are four main routes running east and west, along with two southerly loops and seven crossover trails. Envision a ladder and you've got the basic idea. All trails spread out in ladder-rung fashion. Longer east–west routes form each side of the ladder heading west from the lodge, with the rung connectors between them at intervals close enough that if you get tired, you can head back on one of them. Skiers used to more-difficult-rated routes can easily handle most of the loops, but a few areas are for advanced striders only. The area used to groom for skating skiers, but has stopped because of lack of demand. Owner Cool says you could theoretically ski every loop—that's about 25 kilometers of trails—without seeing the main lodge, yet never be more than 1.2 kilometers away from it.

Families with kids can head west from the lodge to the first north–south crossing, then take the first trail crossing to your left to

Directions at a glance

KILOMETER

0.0 Head west from lodge.

0.6 Turn left at first north–south intersection.

0.12 Continue through two trail intersections.

0.24 Turn left at trail intersection.

1.0 Return to lodge.

Other trails radiate in ladder-rung fashion from start.

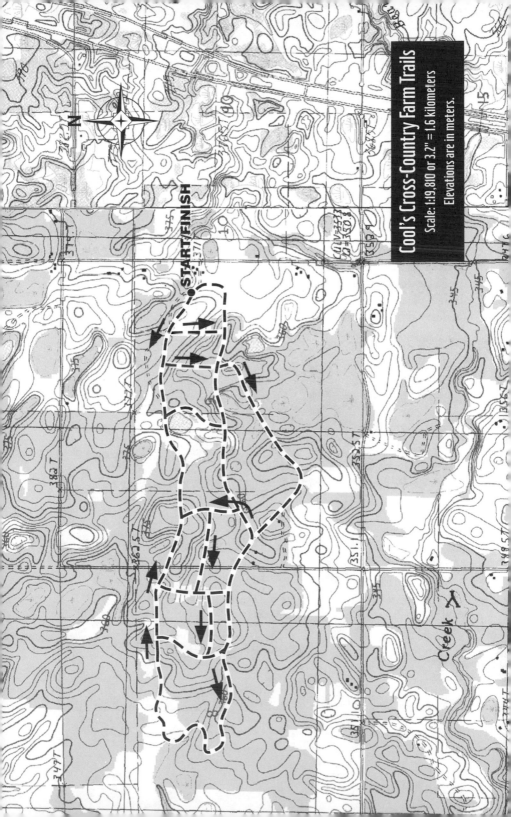

Cool's Cross-Country Farm Trails
Scale: 1:19,810 or 3.2" = 1.6 kilometers
Elevations are in meters.

START/FINISH

Creek

head back for a nice, easy run of about an hour. Without kids, it'll probably take about 10 minutes. You'll have gone probably 1 kilometer over easy terrain.

Go the other way and you're in for a good ascent of Bald Mountain, a hefty 300-foot climb that will tax the legs and stamina of any expert. The view from the top is worth it, as is knowing you've just climbed within 200 feet of Lower Michigan's highest elevation. If you've got the energy and know-how, you might like to run down the face of the hill. One of the few named runs starts from the top as well. Lobo Run twists and turns downhill through 0.5 kilometer of forest almost due south from the top. It's more than a bit hairy. A new trail constructed for the 1999–2000 season starts at the top and goes down the northern side, dropping into a little swampy area before heading back up to the top. It's a good 1-kilometer roller-coaster ride.

One of the most popular routes will take you between numbered points of interest on the trail map, from 1 to 12. Skiers who can handle at least more-difficult trails can take this one for about 8 kilometers

The main lodge at Cool's Cross-Country Farm was built of wood cut from the property.

through a variety of terrain and sights. Some of the points of interest include the hemlock stand surrounding marker 1 on the second north–south connector route—Lobo Run—you'll encounter. It's one of the most picturesque spots in the system; it has been left virtually untouched, because hemlock does not make good lumber. You might see deer yarding up in these trees, which provide good cover from the weather.

Continue west through the center of the trails, across 220th Avenue—there's usually enough snow to ski right across the road—to Nichol's Farm, a 120-year-old farm homestead, the only remnants of which are the holes that formed the foundations of the home and barn, and what's left of the original apple orchard, which deer like to frequent.

Technical skiers should try the inner southern loop, which heads past marker 3. Reach it by heading south from Lake Arthur, a man-made lake in a former cedar swamp. The trail runs diagonally from northeast to southwest to the Big Pine, a virgin white pine that's an example of Michigan's state tree, one of two that escaped 19th-century lumbermen because it was too small to cut back then. In 1999 the top of one of the trees was toppled by a storm, and the tree had to be cut; only the stump remains. The second one still towers above the surrounding maple forest, however.

At the far western edge of the property is the beaver basin, your chance to see what a beaver pond looks like. The flat-tails have been so successful that the Cools had to reroute part of the trail a few years ago when it became inundated with the pond.

The Cools say that since the trail map and system here are different from those at a lot of other operations, it might take you a visit or two to get used to them. They've made excellent use of this relatively small chunk of land to provide an outstanding ski experience.

Big M Cross Country Ski Area Trails
Manistee National Forest, Manistee

Trail type: ━━━ 🌀

Location: Off MI 55, 14 miles east of Manistee. Take it to Udell Hills Road, then drive 3.5 miles south to the lodge area. Trails are within the Manistee National Forest. The access road is paved, and the parking lot is plowed.

Also used by: Generally no one. Snowmobiles aren't allowed, but since this is public land, you'll spot the occasional hiker. Snowshoers using the ski trails are welcome, but please stay off the track.

Distance: 30 kilometers, all for striding. Single track set.

Terrain: Level, gently winding trails for beginners, moderate and varied terrain on intermediate trails, and fast, big trails for advanced skiers, with vertical rises and drops of up to 150 feet. The area gets up to 150 inches of snow a year because it's within the Lake Michigan lake-effect snowbelt.

Trail dificulty: Easiest to most difficult, with a few trails rated challenge routes because they are especially tricky, mostly due to the hills.

Surface quality: Groomed weekly or as necessary. Trails are generally unidirectional, but some sections are two-way. Going one-way here is not crucial because traffic is light, especially on weekdays.

Food and facilities: Pit toilets are available at the site, and a log warming shelter is found at the parking lot. Trail fees are voluntary; the suggested donation is $5.00 per day for nonmembers. Memberships range from $15.00 to $50.00 annually. No funds are received from any governmental source, and all fees go for upkeep, grooming, and maintenance. Accommodations include the Best Western Manistee, with 72 rooms, an indoor pool, and a restaurant, and the Wellston Inn, east of Manistee in the tiny town of Wellston off MI 55, 6 miles from Big M. Restaurants include River Street Station downtown on the Manistee River. Ski rentals are available at Northwind Sports in Manistee. There's a hospital in Manistee.

Phone numbers: Information on Big M is on the Internet at www.
westmichigan.net/bigm. Trail conditions, (231) 723–6121,
ext. 160. Best Western Manistee, (231) 723–9949. Wellston
Inn, (231) 848–4163. River Street Station, (231) 723–8411.
Northwind Sports, (231) 723–2255. For more on the general
area, contact the Manistee Area Convention and Visitors
Bureau, (231) 723–7975 or (800) 288–2286; Web site,
www.manistee~edo.chamber.

A BOOMING LOCAL downhill ski area until the early 1970s, when someone
overbuilt it and it went bust, Big M has hosted legions of dedicated cross-
country skiers since 1984, when the Manistee Cross-Country Ski Council cut most of the trails that now exist. The result is a great collection of
paths that cut through the hardwood highlands east of Lake Michigan.
The council maintains the runs today, along with a log warming lodge
heated by a woodstove at the trailhead and parking lot. All trail intersections are numbered so you'll know where you are when you look at the
trail map. The council has taken care not to scare skiers half to oblivion
by making their trails so difficult they can only be handled by experts. Even
on most-difficult-rated loops with hills, most steeps have straight runouts.

Everyone starts out a beginner here, on either Corkpine, a 2.2-kilome-
ter trail that squiggles and curls through the trees to the south, or Lumberjack, at 2.8 kilometers, going north. Lumberjack is the entrance route
to the rest of the system. Of course, some never get farther than these two
trails, which are generally very flat and cut through the hardwoods.

As you go north on Lumberjack, however, you can take a shortcut to
your left back to the parking lot or onto Double Bit (more on this later),
but most can continue northward. This trail continues along a fairly flat
section until just before doubling back. There's a hill that drops about 25
feet—it may be more than a beginner wants to tackle—then doubles
back toward the lodge. If you prefer to miss the hill, you'll find the first
of several bypasses on the system that take you around the largest elevation drops. At marker 3 head south. You can then go west at marker 7
onto Ryberg Road, a 2.7-kilometer easiest-rated track that loops back to
Lumberjack. It then goes back south to the lodge.

If you're a skier who likes a bit of adventure, turn left at marker 2
instead of continuing north. It will take you to the lower portion of Double Bit. Head west from here. Your destination is Catamount, a 6.2-kilo-
meter most-difficult-rated run to the southwest.

On the way you might want to take the first challenge route you'll
encounter to Dave's Lookout, named for ski council member Dave

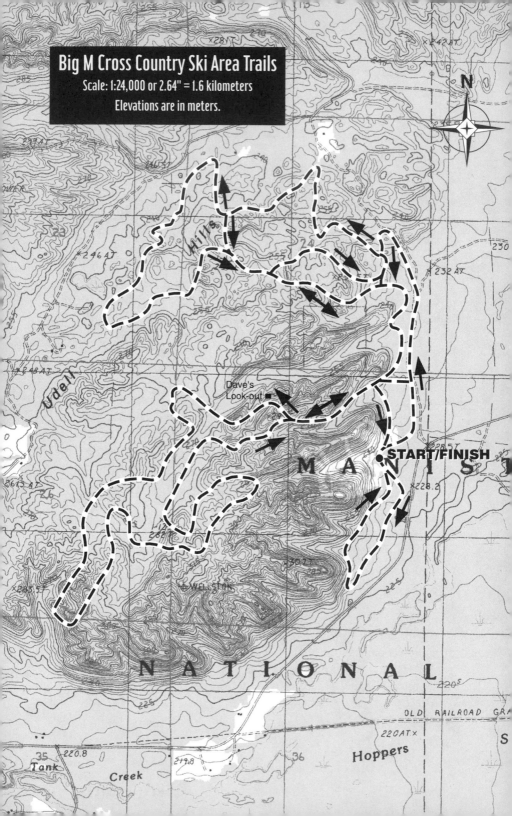

Big M Cross Country Ski Area Trails
Scale: 1:24,000 or 2.64" = 1.6 kilometers
Elevations are in meters.

N

Dave's
Look-out

START/FINISH

M A N I S

N A T I O N A L

Udell

Wellston

Tank

Creek

Hoppers

OLD RAILROAD GRA

220 AT x

Yarnell. You'll squeeze through the trees on this ungroomed, skier-set track for about 60 feet up to a scenic lookout, where you can see for several miles across the surrounding forest. All the way to the lookout and past it, you'll be climbing slightly, but you'll appreciate this later on the return trip.

Beyond Dave's continue through some fairly steep hills between marker 11 and 10, then make a hard left at marker 10 to join Catamount. You'll almost immediately encounter a set of steep uphills and downhills up to 30 feet high. There's another bypass around these two humps. From there the trail gets wavy with ups and downs; what climbing there is, is interspersed with downhills.

At the southern end of Catamount, stop to look out over another scenic view. On clear days you can see all the way to Manistee, about 14 miles away. Hang on from here, because there's a sharp left and then an elevator drop of about 50 feet, followed by a series of smaller bumps along a ridgeline. At marker 13 you can follow the ridge to Capper's Peak, actually the top of what used to be the downhill runs overlooking the lodge. You can go down from there but it's not recommended because the forest service has placed posts in the hill to discourage dirt bikes and four-wheel-drive vehicles from tearing it up in summer. So turn around and go back. At marker 13 you can either take another bypass or prepare to tackle Catamount's largest downhill, a wide-open drop of about 40 feet around a gradual left-hand turn. Shortly after, there's another 20-foot downhill. The trail turns right to the last bypass area, where two 20-footers await. Once you make it past this and you're headed back eastward on Double Bit, you can rest, because it's a nice gradual downhill glide nearly back to the lodge with little or no poling. If the snow's good, it's a good run. If it's icy, it can be fast.

Thrill seekers who want to challenge the biggest drop can head for Camp 24 Trail, a 3.6-kilometer more-difficult roller coaster named for an old logging camp. It's the connection with Oh Me II, a 4.9-kilometer most-difficult trail at marker 5. Take the challenge route for a very steep screamer of about 40 feet. The normal route onto Oh Me is more forgiving but still an exciting ride down. There are three other large hills on Oh Me before it turns back to Camp 24.

Directions at a glance

KILOMETER

0.0 From lodge turn onto Corkpine, one of several loops.

1.1 Trail turns sharply to return to lodge.

2.2 Return to lodge.

Other more-difficult routes lead from lodge northward.

TIPS BEFORE YOUR TRIP

Make sure you have a great time on the slopes by preparing yourself and the family properly. Follow these tips:

■ Always warm up before hitting the trail by stretching, especially your leg ligaments.

■ Don't ski alone or without letting someone know where you're going and when you'll be back. Most of Michigan's ski trails are not patrolled.

■ Layer your clothing, and always have dry clothes to put on when you're done. I guarantee that you'll be sweaty when you return. Always wear a hat (yes, kids, a hat). Up to 70 percent of your body heat is lost through the head if it's uncovered. Loss of body heat could lead to hypothermia. Mittens are always warmer than gloves.

■ On longer trips, take matches, tissue paper, fluids, and a compass. Always carry a trail map.

■ You can get a worse sunburn on bright days in the woods than you can at the beach. Bring plenty of sunscreen.

Here's where many skiers should exercise caution. The point where Oh Me turns right onto Camp 24 is probably Big M's most dangerous step-down, recording more injuries than any other spot. You can either take the bypass there or head down, but it's deceiving terrain, with its undulating stair steps—a series of little bumps where you don't expect them that can easily throw you off balance. Once past these you're back on either Double Bit from marker 6 going south or the easiest-rated Ryberg Road, which connects with Lumberjack for an easy cruise back to your vehicle.

Remember that like most routes through the Michigan forest, these are not safety-swept at the end of each day, so it's always best to ski with a partner.

Crystal Mountain Resort Trails
Crystal Mountain Resort, Thompsonville

Trail type: ▬ ◄ ●

Notes: Includes two dedicated snowshoe trails and the Michigan Legacy Art Park with original outdoor art. Guided snowshoe hikes Saturday evening.

Location: Thompsonville, 28 miles southwest of Traverse City and about 40 miles northwest of Cadillac along MI 115.

Also used by: No one.

Distance: 40 kilometers, including 6 kilometers of lighted trails. There's 4.5 kilometers of snowshoe routes.

Terrain: Crystal sits along the edge of a large, glacial ridgeline, with golf courses making up most of the flat areas and some valleys, which are also used by Nordic skiers. Elevation changes run up to 400 vertical feet. The ridge is covered with hardwoods, while the fairways are lined with trees but generally open. The terrain is deceiving, however; the most-difficult ratings are there for a reason.

Trail dificulty: Easiest to most difficult

Surface quality: All trails groomed for both striding and skating. Half of the loops are two-way. Easiest and more-difficult trails are generally double track set.

Food and facilities: Crystal is a full-service ski resort with 212 rooms, more than 80 chalets, an indoor pool, a lounge with weekend entertainment, and a restaurant. Other restaurants and smaller accommodations are nearby, mostly along MI 115. Trail fees run $11.00 for adults; $32.00 for a family of up to four; $8.00 after 5:00 P.M. For ages 13–18 fees are $8.00 all day, $6.00 after 5:00 P.M.; children 6 and under are free. Rental fees for skating or striding run $6.00 for ages 13 and up, $12.00 for ages 7–12, and $5.00 for ages 6 and under. Telemark skis cost $27.00 daily for ages 13 and up, $20.00 for ages 7–12. Snowshoes run $16.00 daily, $13.00 for four hours, or $8.00 for two hours. Pulk rentals are $20.00 daily, $17.00 for four hours, and $8.00 for two hours. Lessons are also available. The Nordic center is open 9:00 A.M. to 7:00 P.M. Sunday through Thursday, 9:00 A.M. to 9:00 P.M. Friday and Saturday. There are hospitals in Traverse City and Cadillac.

Phone numbers: Call Crystal Mountain, (800) YOUR–MTN, for lodging and ski conditions.

WANT A FAMILY-FRIENDLY ski resort? You've come to the right place. Crystal prides itself on making young families feel at home, whether it's in a slopeside lodge room, the village homes in the woods, or one of the hot condos perched amid the trees along the western edge of the property.

Crystal completed upgrading its trails for the 1999–2000 season, simplifying signage and marking intersections to coincide with numbers on the trail map, which is always a good thing. The resort also is a new Fischer Key Nordic Center, with ski demos and state-of-the-art rental equipment available.

The mountain's most skier-friendly trail combo is Aspen/Nepsa (Aspen spelled backward, since that's how you'll return if you're not in the mood for climbing), rated more difficult for all of its 13.2 kilometers. It traverses a golf course at first, then strays into the wooded boonies a bit. Once you begin there is no exit or shortcut back to the start; you can only turn around, because this is a two-way loop. It's Crystal's longest trail, and it ends with a long, winding climb to an overlook of the beautiful Betsie River Valley and state forestland.

Start off from the Cross Country Center at the far western side of the downhill runs. You'll leave along Stag Hollow, a gentle beginner's trail and the main thoroughfare departing the center along the edge of the downhill runs. There's a very gradual uphill rise of about 25 feet as you traverse one of the golf course fairways. Stag Hollow veers right. Keep going straight.

Cross a road and head through a beautifully wooded stretch that's now called Jack's Rabbit, another easiest-rated trail that's actually a golf cart path for the resort's Betsie Valley Golf Course. You'll be entering more hardwoods as you go farther here until you reach another trail branch. This is the first of two opportunities you have to cut your trip short before you head into the woods. You can decide which to take—continuing straight on Jack's Rabbit or heading immediately onto Aspen/Nepsa by turning left into the forest paralleling two Mountain Ridge Golf Course fairways. The latter is the way most folks go. If you

Directions at a glance

KILOMETER

0.0   All trails start from Cross Country Center, leaving on Stag Hollow.

1.0   Go straight at first intersection and cross road.

2.0   Turn left onto Aspen/Nepsa.

3.0   Turn right onto Jack's Rabbit to return to center.

4.0   Continue through intersection.

5.0   Cross road and continue on to center.

6.0   Reach center.

Other trails expand into the hardwood hills surrounding downhill runs.

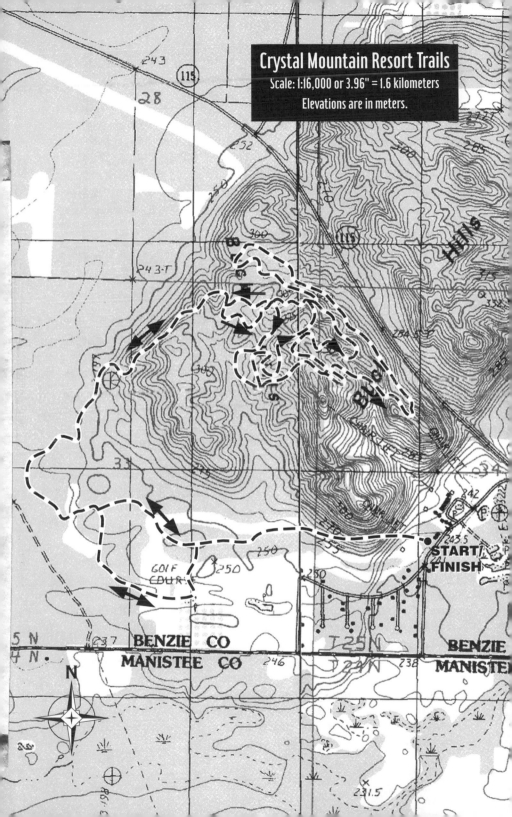

Crystal Mountain Resort Trails
Scale: 1:16,000 or 3.96" = 1.6 kilometers
Elevations are in meters.

Crystal Mountain is known for well-groomed skating trails.

do, you'll be tested a bit already. Paralleling the Mountain Ridge seventh fairway, you'll be gliding downhill a bit on your way with a few ups and downs and a total drop of about 75 feet, but no major headaches.

You'll finally meet back up with Jack's Rabbit. Continue left to stay on Aspen/Nepsa. You're now in a mixed hardwood and pine plantation away from the golf course where it's pretty flat for quite a way. Near the Mountain Ridge 14th hole, however, things change. The trail crosses a series of undulating roller-coaster hills here and there, with falls and climbs of around 25 vertical feet.

Then things get even more interesting after you leave the Mountain Ridge 15th and head into the woods. Where the route turns one-way, more for safety than for any other reason. You're beginning a long climb of up to 200 vertical feet. There are several plateaus to give you some relief, however, and get you prepared for what's next. If you choose to make a hard left, you'll then be headed down on an adventurous little trip. There's quite a windy switchback off the fall line that drops a quick

75 feet. It keeps intermediates on their toes, because there's a bend or two in the trail as you lose elevation. From there you'll encounter a more gradual downhill run and end up back in the pines, where the trail flattens out again to merge with the other part of Aspen/Nepsa you were on to get to the whoop-de-do part.

If you choose not to come back down this way, you can get to the very top of the ridge by heading up higher, cruising up part of the Mountain Ridge 16th on your way to Doe's Delight. Follow this up to the top through some moderate terrain climbs of around 50 feet until finally, you're rewarded with a spectacular view of the Betsie Valley for miles around. From this point it's all downhill as you run a fairly gradual 75-foot drop alongside Mountain Ridge's 17th fairway. At the bottom let your skis run, because you've met up with the top leg of Stag Hollow, the trail you started out on from the center. It's a nice, restful downhill glide all the way back, except for one side road crossing.

Hot shots and those who aspire to be are advised to dump off at the start of Stag Hollow's downhill bent and head left for Glacier Valley/Screaming Eagle, a 6.6-kilometer "experience." Screaming Eagle is the most adrenaline-testosterone-soaked loop at Crystal. There are never-ending uphills and bad-tempered downhills that are a featured attraction on one of the resort's four black-diamond-rated cross-country trails.

It starts with a climb of at least 250 feet without a break through the woods that takes even experienced racers a good 8 to 10 minutes to tackle. Once that's over, Screaming Eagle heads off straight right, while Glacier Valley jogs left. Head right as the trail plays along the ridgeline overlooking MI 115. Then hang on as it drops precipitously through a hairpin. You'll drop about 90 feet to a manageable U-turn that leads to yet another climb up the ridge where you'll be winding in and out of hardwoods.

At the power line you'll head into an off-camber turn into a steep downhill where the trail cuts back hard to the left. It's called the Hannenkham, a treacherous 180-degree turn that's tough to handle because you'll be carrying quite a bit of speed when you get there. If you're an extremely avid skier, you can step-turn into it, but most skid through, or try to. Look for lots of sitzmarks here from those who didn't make it. After that one you'll begin a slight vertical climb, then another downhill that parallels MI 115. This part of the trail serpentines in and out, climbing and dropping, with no real time to rest in between. There's another steep climb of about 80 feet to a point where the trail steers a bit to the north. Most skiers can have all they can handle by herringboning to the top, then hanging on for a steep, treacherous downhill with a sharp left-hander to handle while all the time dropping about 100 vertical feet.

Then guess what? Another gradual, unforgiving climb of at least 200 vertical feet. You'll cross the power line again to reach the top of the ridge you started on. Following some nice whoop-de-dos, there's an 80-foot downhill run back to the bottom, where you can thankfully exit for Nepsa or a shorter route, Doe's Delight. This is a tough route, used for the Michigan Cup and Crystal relay races.

The resort's two lighted trails are Stag Hollow and Otter Run, a 2.6-kilometer loop at the far eastern end of the complex that circles several Betsie Valley course fairways. Trails are lighted with low-wattage lamps so you can still see the stars. They're open until 10:00 p.m. daily. Otter is used as a cross-country teaching trail.

The resort's two snowshoe trails are nice, easy tromps through the woods totaling 4.5 kilometers. Stomp Way is very flat and perfect for families. Pineapple heads off Stomp Way across County Line Road to make a big circle through the woods.

Head to your right and cross two side roads to reach Crystal's unique Michigan Legacy Art Park. Also accessible by a most-difficult ski trail, the park was developed in 1991 and features upward of two dozen artworks of steel, wood, and stone pertaining to Michigan history, all by Michigan artists. The park is ever evolving, because some works are created on the spot. It is as much a must-see as Crystal's trails are a must-do.

Sand Lakes Quiet Area Trails

Sand Lakes Quiet Area, Traverse City

Trail type: ━━ ⬤

Location: 15 miles east of Traverse City. From MI 72 head southward at the signs on Broomhead Road about 6 miles to the parking lot.

Also used by: Occasional winter hikers and campers.

Distance: Seven loops of 2 to 8 miles.

Terrain: Glacial hills that can be up to 50 feet in elevation, mixed with lots of flats. Trails are too narrow for skating. The area is heavily wooded, from regenerated trees to mature old-growth timber, with hardwoods like maple and oak predominant.

Trail dificulty: Easiest to more difficult.

Surface quality: All trails are ungroomed, because no motorized vehicles are allowed in the quiet area, but the routes get enough traffic that there are generally skier-set tracks.

Food and facilities: There are pit toilets at the trailhead parking lot. Restaurants and motels are available west toward Traverse City, including Grand Traverse Resort, a high-rise full-service complex with 669 rooms, suites, and condos, along with a health club and restaurants. Lots of other, less expensive motels and restaurants are located along MI 72 in Traverse City, and to the east in Kalkaska. Rentals are available in Traverse City. The Traverse City Convention and Visitors Bureau can send you brochures on the entire area covering other places to stay and eat, and things to do when you're not skiing. Hospitals are found in Traverse City and Kalkaska.

Phone numbers: Grand Traverse Resort, (231) 938–2100 or (800) 748–0303. Traverse City Convention and Visitors Bureau, (231) 947–1120 or (800) 872–8377. For trail conditions call (231) 922–5280 weekdays.

THIS IS ONE of the most popular ski areas in the region, yet it also feels like one of the most remote, depending on where you are on the system. The quiet area gets its name from the fact that no motorized vehicles are allowed in this 2,800-acre tract within the Pere Marquette State Forest. Only foot and bike travel are allowed.

That indescribable roaring silence is appreciated only when you experience it. The only sounds are of the wind rustling through the trees and your skis gliding on snow, except for the occasional airplane. Tree roots help create tiny rolling bumps over much of the way, but in general terrain is delightfully not too difficult and perfect for day skiers or families with small children. All routes are marked with numerals corresponding to trail intersections.

For a good trek from the parking lot, ski between the intersections in the following route. It's not very hilly and takes you past three of the quiet area's lakes. You'll have completed a good 2.3-mile tour that you'll want to come back to hike in summer.

Start out from the parking lot. About 0.8 mile later you'll be deep into the woods at marker 2. Turn left for the short trek to 3, where you'll turn right again to 4, heading into the prettiest parts of the quiet area. This section of trail is fairly flat but beautiful just the same. At 3 the trail makes a sharp right turn to the south, skirting Lake 3, one of a cluster of five lakes in this part of the woods all named by numbers. Lake 2 is a designated trout lake. Lake 3 is between markers 4 and 16.

From here to the next intersection is 0.6 mile through gorgeous woods. At marker 16 you'll want to make a right turn to stay on this leg.

Directions at a glance

MILE

0.0 From parking lot enter trail system.

0.9 Turn right at marker 2.

1.0 Continue to marker 3.

1.2 Continue to marker 4.

1.8 Continue to marker 16. Turn right.

2.6 Turn right at marker 17.

3.0 Turn left toward marker 2 at marker 18.

3.1 Turn left at marker 2.

4.0 Return to lot.

It meanders northwest for 0.75 mile through the woods again until it reaches marker 17, the site of an old fire lane that cut the quiet area in half from east to west. Between this intersection and the next at 18, and back on to 4, you'll start to hit some moderate rolling hills of 10 to 20 feet in elevation in an area of mature hardwoods.

More-advanced skiers might want to try the quiet area's great circle route, a trek of about 8.3 miles that encompasses the entire area and will send you into some pretty remote stretches where you can enjoy that wilderness feeling only a few miles from two of northern Michigan's largest towns. A well and pit toilet at marker 5, alongside Lake 1, are open depending on the weather. Head up through markers 6 and 8, past a small pond at marker 9, then through a series of tight turns and hills that can be tricky if you don't know they're coming. At marker 10 you'll be heading south through beautiful woods. At marker 14 meet up with

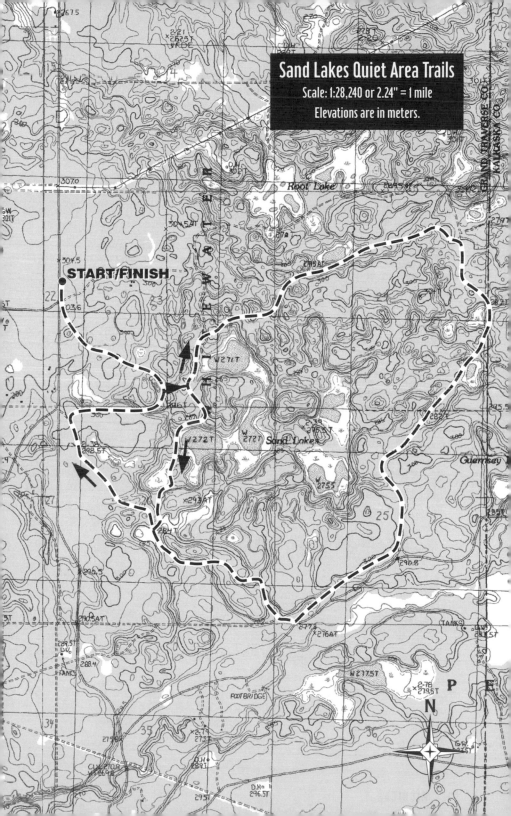

Sand Lakes Quiet Area Trails
Scale: 1:28,240 or 2.24" = 1 mile
Elevations are in meters.

START/FINISH

the Cross-Michigan Riding and Hiking Trail, which heads across the state from Empire on the western side to end close to the Tawas area's Corsair Trail Complex (see separate entry under East Michigan).

You'll also be only a few short strides from the North Branch of the Boardman River, which eventually empties into Grand Traverse Bay at Traverse City. Head west a bit on the riding trail until the next intersection, where you'll meet with marker 15. That will take you up to 16 and the route as previously described. Except for a few spots, this is a pretty moderate trek as far as hills go, but the distance is what will get you. The trek is definitely not for beginners.

Hill lovers can head off for the area's interior by taking the route from 6 and 7 to 15, then from 16, 17, and 18 back to 4, then turning left back toward the start. Between markers 6 and 15 are probably the area's largest hills, up to 50 feet and ambitious climbs. As is the case on all the routes here, the way down is pretty narrow through the trees, so stay in control or the downhill ride could get you in trouble.

The Sand Lakes Quiet Area is a Michigan gem that isn't visited too often, and once you've been here to enjoy the stillness of the woods and the solitude, you'll be glad that your fellow skiers and hikers want to keep it that way.

Muncie Lakes Pathway

Pere Marquette State Forest, Traverse City

Trail type: ▬▬▬

Location: In the Pere Marquette State Forest, southeast of downtown Traverse City, on Ranch Rudolph Road off Garfield Road. The easiest way to get there is to head south from Traverse City on Garfield Road. Turn east onto Ranch Rudolf Road to the parking lot on the northern side of the highway. The pathways are named for the lakes in the northwestern corner of the system.

Also used by: The occasional winter horseback rider on one section of trail.

Distance: 9.8 miles on five loops that stretch out in ladder-rung form from the parking lot.

Terrain: The countryside consists of rolling to moderate to higher hills. There are quick elevation changes of up to 50 feet. Some spots on the trail reach higher, but they are relatively gradual with no sharp turns. Some of the loops go close to the Boardman River.

Trail dificulty: Easiest to most difficult.

Surface quality: Groomed weekly, weather permitting, generally prior to each weekend. Single track set. All trails are two-way, but there is a suggested direction. Intersection markers correspond to numbers on trail maps so you can locate your position easily. Segments of the trail cross a road five times.

Food and facilities: There is a unisex bathroom at the parking lot. The area is located only a few miles from Traverse City's motels and hotels. Most are located along U.S. 31 generally east of downtown, with scores to choose from. The Traverse City Convention and Visitors Bureau can send you brochures on the entire area covering where to stay and eat, and things to do when you're not skiing. There's a hospital in Traverse City.

Phone numbers: Traverse City Convention and Visitors Bureau, (231) 947–1120 or (800) 872–8377. For trail conditions, call (231) 922–5280 weekdays.

THIS IS ONE of the most popular trail systems in the Traverse City region because of its proximity to the city and the fact that all loops are groomed. You'll find the area covered with beautiful hardwoods, and you'll be skiing in and out of the Boardman River Valley, the same trout stream that flows through downtown Traverse City before emptying into Grand Traverse Bay. A trip along this route will give you a bit of an idea why the Traverse region is the largest metro area in northern Lower Michigan.

Muncie Lakes Pathway
Scale: 1:29,550 or 2.14" = 1 mile
Elevations are in meters.

Because the first loop is rated easiest, it's one of the more popular for skiers who want a quick, woodsy, and easy jaunt. Go out via markers 1 and 2, then veer left. About 0.75 mile later you'll run into marker 3. Turn right and go 0.4 mile to 12, then head right again for the 0.6 mile leg back to 2. This is hardwood country, and you'll set a lot on this great beginner's loop.

If you're looking for a more-difficult-rated run with a few more moderate hills that's still not too difficult, head straight instead of turning at marker 3. Again, nothing too hard, just increased distance. Turn right at marker 4 and you'll be on a hill with the Boardman below, at marker 11, where you'll turn right for home and parallel the river valley back to the start.

The northern trails get harder, but there are some ways to beat the hills if you wish, at least for a while, by heading in the direction of the river valley, not away from it. First, though, try the suggested route.

Leaving from marker 3, head to 4, a more-difficult-rated 0.8-mile segment that climbs about 30 feet overall. Continue straight from 4 for 0.4 mile on more-difficult trail to marker 5. You can either take a shortcut between 5 and 7 or turn left into the heart of the Muncie Lakes, skirting the shores of two before looping back east across a power line. They won't look much like lakes, just snow-covered open areas. From there it's a straight run east to markers 7 and 8. At 8 prepare to submerge, because you'll be heading up and down hills. First you'll head up a long, gradual 50 feet then make a steep drop back into the river valley, or you can avoid the valley and take the shortcut from 8 to 10. Between markers 8 and 9 there's a steep one—a good 75-footer—while you'll be curving right and joining up with the Michigan Shore to Shore Riding and Hiking Trail about halfway down.

Directions at a glance

MILE
0.0   From lot leave on trail.
0.1   Turn left at marker 2.
0.9   Continue through marker 3.
1.7   Turn right at marker 4.
2.4   Turn right at marker 11.
3.3   Continue through marker 12.
3.9   Continue through marker 2 to return to lot.

You'll hit bottom only a short way from the river's edge at marker 9. Rest here for a bit before your next challenge—climbing back up the ridge you just came down. Between markers 9 and 10 is a 1.1-mile segment that's uphill nearly all the way, hence its most-difficult rating. And unless you want to bust a trail along the river, it's the only way you can go.

At marker 10 turn south. The trail again follows the ridgeline with some undulating smaller ups and downs for 1.1 miles to marker 11, then back to marker 12. It's all rated more difficult and you'll be following the valley ridge all the way back. Make this trek and you'll have done the Muncie and yourself proud.

Lake Ann Pathway
Lake Ann State Forest, Traverse City

Trail type: ▬▬▬

Location: On the western side of Lake Ann on Reynolds Road north of U.S. 31, 15 miles west of Traverse City. From U.S. 31 go north on Lake Ann Road. At Lake Ann turn west onto Almira Road, then south onto Reynolds Road, which goes past the Lake Ann State Forest Campground, the location of the trailhead. Parking is on the eastern side of the road, near the lake, and loops are found on both sides of the road.

Also used by: No one.

Distance: Four loops with 5.8 miles of trails. Trails are two-way, and numbered posts corresponding to numbers on the trail map mark intersections. However, most visitors tend to follow the trails counterclockwise.

Terrain: Routes range between level on the eastern side of Reynolds Road to gently rolling on the western segment, where it's a bit hillier, with elevation changes of 30 to 50 feet. The entire area is wooded. The western side is gently rolling to rolling hills, all wooded, with heights of 30 to 50 feet. Most beginners will want to stay on the eastern side.

Trail dificulty: Easiest to most difficult.

Surface quality: Ungroomed, but generally skier-set tracks.

Food and facilities: There is a campground on the site open in summer. Pit toilets may be open and the hand pump may work, depending on the weather. There are scores of accommodations along with restaurants open in Traverse City to the east, and in Honor, along U.S. 31, to the west. The Traverse City Convention and Visitors Bureau can send you brochures on the entire area covering where to stay and eat, and things to do when you're not skiing. There's a hospital in Traverse City.

Phone numbers: Traverse City Convention and Visitors Bureau, (231) 947–1120 or (800) 872–8377. For trail conditions, call (231) 922–5280 weekdays.

WHILE NOT AS challenging as some of its neighboring routes, Lake Ann is becoming a popular system because of its variety, proximity to Traverse City, and great lake, river, and forest scenery. Part of the trail not only goes along the shore of Lake Ann, measuring about a mile wide north–south and east–west, but also meanders along two other smaller waters and a stretch of the Platte River, one of the prettiest trout streams in this part of

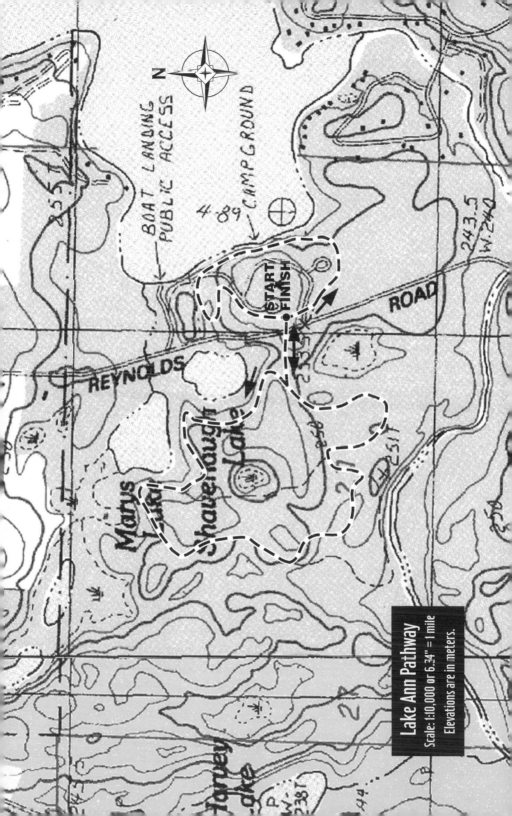

N

BOAT LANDING
PUBLIC ACCESS

CAMPGROUND

4.89

255.7

243.5
W.240

START
FINISH

ROAD

REYNOLDS

Shauenaugh Lake

Marys Lake

Torney Lake

Lake Ann Pathway
Scale: 1:10,000 or 6.34" = 1 mile
Elevations are in meters.

Michigan. The river bottom is so pebbly in areas that it looks golden. In fall visitors come up to a stretch of stream south of U.S. 31 to fish for migrating salmon, and they do so again in spring for steelhead, a lake-run type of rainbow trout. In summer the river opens to stream trout anglers, too.

As you leave the parking lot area at post 2, beginners can head south to post 3 along an extremely gradual downhill slope as the trail heads toward the river. At marker 3 you can also turn left to return north along the Lake Ann shore before looping to your left and making an ess turn to eventually get back to the lot.

Take this shortcut and you'll have gone 1.2 miles. Continue and the entire trip will cover about 1.8 miles. The river is a great place to stop. It's a fast-flowing, pebble-bottomed stream that runs clear and cold along cedar "sweepers" and other trees. This is a great easiest-rated trail, and you'll be skiing the edges of the state forest campground over smallish hills and some open lakefront land.

Once you've gotten your skis warmed up, take them off to cross Reynolds Road if there isn't enough snow and head out on the three loops in the area's western side. They cover 1.1, 1.2, and 3.3 miles, respectively.

Turn right at marker 5 to pass Shavenaugh Lake. You're now on an intermediate-rated trail, but it's still fairly easy, with only a few hills. One of the best things about this system is that even when there are some higher hills, they're fairly easy to negotiate, with no sharp turns at the bottom. You'll veer to the left then head right in a crescent around the lakeshore before taking a hard left toward marker 6.

Directions at a glance

MILE

0.0 From lot turn left at trail inter-section at marker 2.

0.1 Turn left at intersection.

0.9 Continue through intersection.

1.8 Return to lot.

Other loops start across Reynolds Road.

Look to your right and you'll see Mary's Lake on this more-difficult-rated section. The hilliest portions are saved for the farthest loop out, which you can take by veering right at marker 7. Stand by for several bumps of up to 50 feet as the track first climbs, then descends again toward the golden Platte. You'll be about 30 feet from the river, and you can either ski or walk to the banks. From the river you'll be climbing back up and down again to marker 9, but the hills shouldn't be a problem for skiers who've earned their most-difficult ratings. Turn right at 9 to loop along the river valley's ridge on a more-difficult segment down to 10, then go right again back to 5 and the parking lot. Lake Ann may not seem as exciting as trails go because there are few hair-raising runs, but it remains a tranquil trip through the woods and beside both still and rushing waters.

Vasa Trail
Traverse Area Recreational Trails, Acme

Trail type: ▬▬ ◀

Location: In Acme, just east of Traverse City. The trailhead is reached by taking U.S. 31 north from downtown Traverse City. Turn east onto Bunker Hill Road, then south onto Bartlett Road to the start.

Also used by: A snowmobile trail crosses the route three times. No dogs are allowed.

Distance: A total of 38 kilometers of trails, in 25 kilometer, 10 kilometer, and 3 kilometer loops. In other words, if you're not up to a long run, stick with the 3 kilometer or 10 kilometer. There's a shortcut back to the 10 kilometer in the first part of the 25 kilometer loop, if it proves too challenging.

Terrain: Rolling forested hills with some clear-cut open areas. The first part of the trail system is fairly flat. The difficult part comes when you have to climb to the top of a bench of hills. A new trail gets around the hill. The wall is a tough climb, one of the steepest in this region, going about 200 feet up in a short distance—remember, this is a race trail. There are shortcuts, however, that will get you around the worst stuff.

Trail dificulty: Easiest to most difficult.

Surface quality: Groomed at least four times a week, depending on snow conditions. Single and double track set with skating lanes on all trails. Trails are one-way except for the starting segments.

Food and facilities: You'll find a warming shed and rest rooms at the start. The shelter has picnic tables where you can enjoy the snacks or lunch you'll bring. Water and soda pop are available for purchase, but no food. Rentals are available in Traverse City at Brick Wheels. Trail fees are voluntary, but like many Michigan systems, all maintenance of the trails, lodge, and grooming equipment is supported by donations. A donation pipe is at the trailhead. My suggestion is at least $3.00 per person. TART (Traverse Area Recreational Trails), which manages the trail, can be joined for $35.00 (individual) or $50.00 (family) annually. TART also manages summer hiking, biking, and in-line skating trails. There are scores of places to stay and eat in the Traverse City area.

Closest to the trail is Grand Traverse Resort, a high-rise full-service complex with 669 rooms, suites, and condos, along with a health club and restaurants. Lots of other, less expensive motels and restaurants are located along MI 72 in

Traverse City, and to the east in Kalkaska. The Traverse City Convention and Visitors Bureau can send you brochures on the entire area covering where to stay and eat, and things to do when you're not skiing. There's a hospital in Traverse City.

Phone numbers: Traverse City Convention and Visitors Bureau, (231) 947–1120 or (800) 872–8377. For trail conditions, call (231) 922–5280 weekdays. Grand Traverse Resort, (231) 938–2100 or (800) 748–0303. Brick Wheels ski rentals, (231) 947–4274.

IF YOU WANT a comfortable ski through Michigan's hardwood hills outside the northern Lower Peninsula's most popular vacation city, here it is. And if you want a tough, no-holds-barred gut-buster, here it is. Take your choice of three loops that will either please you or test your endurance and make you wonder why you didn't take the shorter route. This is the home of what's probably the peninsula's toughest ski race, the Subaru Vasa, which draws pros and amateurs from across North America. Everything is maintained by donation, so be sure to feed the pipe at the parking lot trailhead.

As you might guess, the 10-kilometer route is the most popular, but quite a few make a day of it on the 25 kilometer, too. I'll tackle the 10 kilometer first.

You'll start off side by side with the 25-kilometer route on a fairly flat portion. This section of the trail is two-way. You'll see one loop that heads off to your right shortly afterward. It's a 3-kilometer classic-skiing-only loop that reconnects with the one you're on a bit later. The 10-kilometer loop bears left a bit then goes over tiny Acme Creek via a bridge. From here on you've got a fairly flat run until your first "little" climb of about 50 feet. It will leave you breathing a bit heavier at the top.

The loop will level off for a short distance, then you'll take one of the trails to your right, which cuts off the majority of the rest of the hill. Go straight to the top to reach a plateau where you can rest on a bench while you ponder which trail to take. Most folks go left to remain on the 10 kilometer. A bit farther on will be time to choose whether to take the 25-kilometer route, or stick to the 10 kilometer.

Directions at a glance

KILOMETER

0.0 Head onto trail at lot.

2.0 Turn left onto trail.

4.0 Turn right at 10 kilometer/25 kilometer split or keep going.

7.0 Turn right.

9.0 Turn left to return to lot.

10.0 Enter parking lot.

The 10 kilometer meanders through the deep hardwoods and over small, relatively gentle rolling hills for about 4 kilometers. Eventually you'll get to the point where the 10-kilometer and 25-kilometer trails

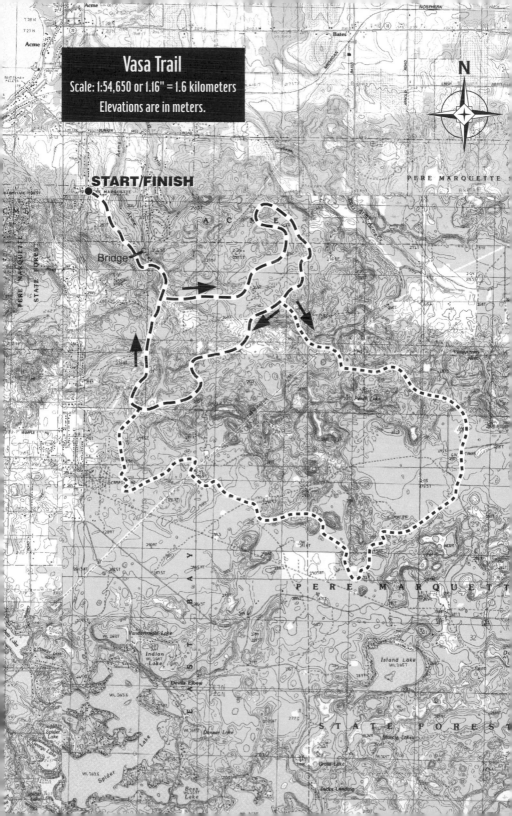

split; there's another rest bench. From here point 'em downhill on the 10 kilometer for a little way. A few minutes later is the bailout shortcut from the 25 kilometer that goes back to the 10 kilometer loop. It's the last chance 25-kilometer skiers have to cut their little jaunt short. Or, if you want, you can also join the 25 kilometer here.

If you keep going on the 10 kilometer, you'll find it fairly flat with intermittent rolling segments while you cross under a power line. Eventually you'll come to a gradual long downhill run that leads to a moderately steep uphill of about 100 feet.

After that the trail levels out and stays flat, then turns back toward the start at the 7 kilometer mark, where it merges for a bit with the 25-kilometer route along a gradual downhill run. From here there's a slight uphill, then the route flattens out with a few rolling hills until you're back at the base of a very steep 200-footer that you don't have to take, thanks to a new bypass at the 8-kilometer mark. It's a short jaunt to the trail back to the trailhead.

If you're up for the 25 kilometer, you've got a few hills to ponder. Where the 10 kilometer leaves, the 25 kilometer cuts back left and, at a wooden-post power line, climbs 50 feet before looping and jogging back. Next comes The Wall, an aptly named, 150-foot, quick, steep ride up followed by rolling terrain. The next landmark, at 11 kilometers, is Big Rock, which is pretty much a big rock. At Jackpine Valley several steep climbs and drops of up to 100 feet await, as the trail jogs first south then north. There are plenty of downhills followed by some hair-raising sharp turns at the bottom, so you might want to take the calmer shortcut that avoids this area altogether. The shortcut will take you through some great scenic woods under a steel power line. The route turns north up to a gut-buster. That same 200-foot hill that plagues the 10- kilometer run is at the 22-kilometer mark, which you can avoid by that new bypass.

If you're an average skier, plan on at least three hours for the 25-kilometer run, and about 90 minutes for the 10 kilometer. If you're a leisurely skier or with the family, plan your longer trip accordingly. Either way, the Vasa Trail will be one of the best experiences of your winter visit to the Traverse City area.

The Vasa Trail travels through scenic stands of pine and hardwoods.

Shanty Creek Resort Trails
Shanty Creek Resort, Mancelona

Trail type: ▬ ◄

Location: At the Shanty Creek Resort complex, west of Mancelona. From U.S. 131 head west on MI 88 to the Schuss Slopes entrance, or continue past Schuss on MI 88. The highway bends north on its way into Bellaire, past the resort's western entrance. Trails start from both the Schuss Slopes and Summit Slopes areas, but the Nordic Ski Center is located at the Schuss base, so most leave from there.

Also used by: No one.

Distance: 30 kilometers in five loops, ranging from 2 kilometers to 22 kilometers from one village to the other.

Terrain: Hilly glacial moraine, wooded with mature maple, beech, and oak. Trails feature gradual elevation changes of up to 350 feet along with great views of the surrounding countryside and Michigan's version of the Finger Lakes.

Trail dificulty: Easiest to most difficult.

Surface quality: Groomed daily. Single track set, and packed for skating. All trails are two-way.

Food and facilities: Lodging is available next to both the Schuss and Summit Slopes, from lodge rooms and condos to rental homes in the woods surrounding both ski areas. There are indoor pools at both locations, along with an outdoor pool at the Schuss Slopes and restaurants at both. Daily trail fees run $12.00 for adults, $8.00 for children ages 12 and under; four-hour passes are $10.00 for adults, $6.00 for ages 12 and under. Ski rentals cost $16.00 per day for ages 13 and up, $12.00 for 12 and under. Four-hour rentals are $12.00 for ages 13 and up, $8.00 for ages 12 and under. Hospitals are found in Kalkaska and Traverse City.

Phone numbers: For accommodations and ski conditions, call Shanty Creek at (800) 678–4111; Web site, www.shantycreek.com.

HERE IS ANOTHER northern Michigan downhill ski area that, unbeknownst to a lot of Nordic skiers, has a collection of trails that are among the best places to learn and grow in your abilities. Much of Shanty's trail system, in fact, is used in the annual White Pine Stampede race the Saturday of the first full weekend in February. There are no trails most-difficult-rated on the system, but that doesn't mean there isn't some beautiful and challenging skiing to be had here. What Shanty lacks in difficulty is more than

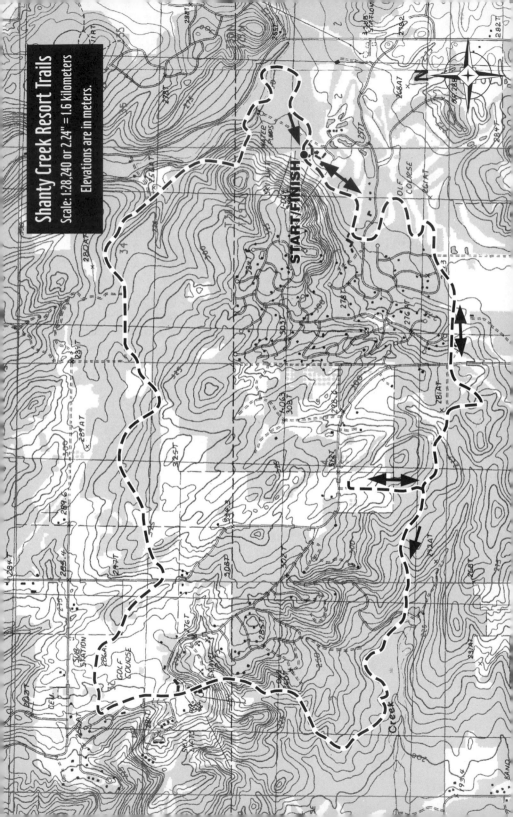

Shanty Creek Resort Trails
Scale: 1:28,240 or 2.24" = 1.6 kilometers
Elevations are in meters.

START/FINISH

made up for in its wonderful views and those soft-as-velvet sunsets over incomparable West Michigan hills.

The resort's two downhill locations, Summit Slopes and Schuss Mountain, actually began as competitors. Free shuttles now take guests between the two, 3 miles apart. Millions of dollars have recently been put into the resort, including Cedar River Village at Schuss Mountain, an 84-suite hotel in the woods within earshot of the Cedar River, where you can start your trail explorations.

Directions at a glance

KILOMETER

0.0 Enter Pine Cone Trail across Schuss Mountain entrance road.

1.0 Cross Schuss Mountain Drive.

1.5 Pass Tamarack Trail entrance.

2.0 Pass Winter Brook Trail entrance.

3.0 Cross service road.

4.0 Turn left to return to Nordic Ski Center.

4.5 Arrive at center.

The Nordic Ski Center is situated near the entrance off Schuss Mountain Drive, which helps connect the two resort complexes. In summer the center is used for Schuss Mountain's golf operations.

Trails around the base of the slopes are very good runs. Most folks push off from the center to start on the 4.5-kilometer Pine Cone Trail, a more-difficult trail that weaves among the hardwoods surrounding the resort's golf course. Heading west from the ski center, Pine Cone follows the fairway cart paths of four different holes, so it's relatively flat here and somewhat open.

Take off your skis and cross Schuss Mountain Drive between holes two and three, and you're headed to Tamarack Trail, a 1.5-kilometer easiest-rated romp through the woods with a nice, gentle uphill climb of about 100 vertical feet. You'll de-ski to cross another road, and then head into an undeveloped hardwood forest until you reach the 2-kilometer Poet's Loop, a well-named more-difficult circular trail that always bears left.

Take a right onto Frog Holler Trail and you'll be going uphill another 100 or so feet until you reach the first sweeping left-hand turn, where you'll ride a plateau until you encounter another left turn and a gradual downhill. Bear left again and you'll parallel MI 88. Ride the flats here until you turn left again and enjoy a gradual downhill drop of 25 feet before you're back at the entrance of Tamarack. Head back to Pine Cone and take it to your right in a large circle around the golf course.

A short link will take you to Shanty's longest route (9 kilometer), Mountain Creek. It's one that figures in as the last leg in the annual Stampede. It's an adventurous little route because it has got some great terrain changes of up to 350 feet from one end to the other and yet is mostly rated more difficult. The best route is to first make the complete trip over to the Summit Slopes side, either via the shuttle or by backtracking on Pine Cone, Tamarack, and Poet's to Frog Holler Trail.

From here you can either pick up a shuttle to the top of Summit at the end of a spur off Frog Holler or continue on to Legend Loop, a 4.3 kilometer more-difficult-rated trail that flows up and over the bumps of up to 50 feet that make up much of Shanty's famed Legend Golf Course.

Then take a chairlift up to the top of the resort, walk to the northern end, and take a look around. To the west looking over the downhill slopes is Michigan's version of the Finger Lakes. Practically each valley you see contains a north–south lake, including Lake Bellaire, larger Torch Lake, and the East Arm of Grand Traverse Bay beyond. You'll start on Mountain Creek heading down a short, steep chute of perhaps 40 feet into a meadow that's the site of another golf course.

Once you get out of the meadows area, you'll head into a straight section locals call the Whoop-De-Dos—a popular name on Michigan trails— a continuous series of eight ups and downs of 20 to 40 feet that is unique to the resort. You'll almost always end up carrying enough speed down one to get up another. On the way down to the Nordic Ski Center at the Schuss side, you'll be passing the gurgling Cedar River, a beautiful, small trout stream bordering the ski area. If you're telemark proficient, you can ride back up to tackle the Schuss slopes or head over to take on the less challenging Summit downhill runs.

Once you're done for the day, relax with dinner at Shanty's Lakeview dining room and watch the lake-effect snows blow in from Lake Michigan across the hills through the picture windows. It's a sight you'll never forget.

Boyne Nordican XC Trail System

Boyne Mountain Ski Area, Boyne Falls

Trail type   ▬ ◀ ⬤

Location: On the grounds of Boyne Mountain Ski Area, located just off U.S. 131 in Boyne Falls, south of Petoskey.

Also used by: Snowshoers are welcome alongside the trails.

Distance: 40 kilometers.

Terrain: Flat to world-class hills, with an elevation change of 450 feet from upper to lower trails. You can descend at whatever speed you wish, either on a dedicated cross-country route or telemarking with the downhillers on the face of the alpine slopes.

Trail dificulty: Easiest to most difficult. Boyne says its trails are 40 percent beginner, 20 percent intermediate, and 40 percent advanced.

Surface quality: Trails closest to the Nordic Center are double track set. The outer trails are single track set with skating lanes. Nearly all trails have skating lanes.

Food and facilities: Trails depart from the resort's separate Nordic Center. Rentals run $12.00 for adults, $7.00 for children ages 8 and under. Short performance skis rent for $15.00 daily and skaters can get on the trail for $20.00 daily. Trail fees of $12.00 per day include a lift ride to the top of the hill for faster access to the main body of trails, and to avoid the gruntwork of a 500-vertical-foot trip up on your slats. Try night skiing for $6.00 on a 3-kilometer lighted trail. Accommodations are available at the resort for 600 guests. Motels in the area include the Brown Trout Motel, with 14 rooms and an indoor pool and whirlpool in Boyne Falls just outside Boyne Mountain Resort. You'll find more choices in Boyne City, just to the north of the resort on Lake Charlevoix. There's dining at the resort, and also in Boyne Falls and nearby Boyne City and other areas around the resort. There's a hospital in Petoskey. The Boyne Country Convention and Visitors Bureau has more information on where to stay and what to do in the general area.

Phone numbers: Call (231) 549–6088 for the Boyne Nordic Center and (800) GO–BOYNE for lodging, and other information on the mountain. Brown Trout Motel, (231) 549–2791. Boyne Country Convention and Visitors Bureau, (800) 845–2858.

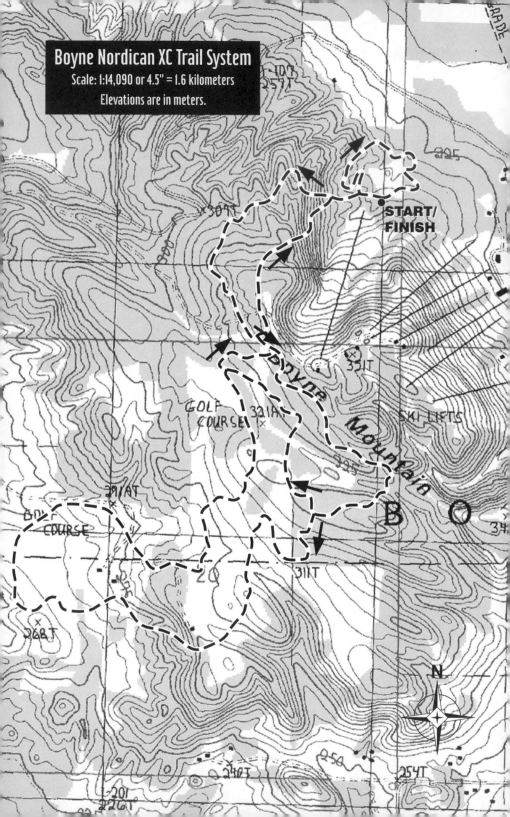

Boyne Nordican XC Trail System
Scale: 1:14,090 or 4.5" = 1.6 kilometers
Elevations are in meters.

START/
FINISH

Canyon Mountain

GOLF
COURSE

GOLF
COURSE

SKI LIFTS

B O

N

MANY FOLKS SKIING the alpine slopes of the northern Lower Peninsula's premier downhill ski area probably wonder just where all those free-wheeling Nordic-type skiers disappear to when they get off the chairlift at the top of the slopes. In fact, they head into the lush hardwoods around one of the state's oldest ski resorts to experience a unique, challenging trail system.

You can either pole your way up nearly 500 feet from the lower trails area or take the Disciples Ridge Chair Lift to the top for an incomparable view of the rolling glacial hills around northwestern Lower Michigan and have the satisfaction that you're about to ski one of the state's best.

The most popular route among veteran skiers is a 15-kilometer jaunt that will bring you a taste of both the lower trails at the base of the downhill runs and the upper routes at the top of the slopes. Start by heading out for a warm-up on Twister, an aptly named 3-kilometer one-way more-difficult loop that zigzags around on a course that looks like a jigsaw puzzle piece, it is so convoluted. Once you've covered it, the macho can tackle the most-difficult run named Little Hammer, which connects with Grinder for the uphill climb to the summit 500 feet above you.

Once you're at the top, catch your breath but prepare to have it taken away again as you look out over a wonderful vista, down at the main lodge area to Boyne and the hills beyond.

From the top follow the signs and the trail around to the left to Vistas, a mellow, more-difficult loop that skirts the top of the mountain ridge and circumnavigates the golf course fairways of the Alpine and Monument links. This is often a great area to ski even if there is no snow on the lower trails. Trust what the Nordic Center folks tell you about this, especially early in the season, when the temperature differential between the top and bottom is surprisingly great. That makes for more snow up top. It's not unusual to have half again as much snow at the top as at the bottom. You'd be amazed what this elevation change does when combined with lake-effect snows. Vistas is reached from that aforementioned improved and repositioned expert run called Grinder, which leads partly up on the ski-run side of

Directions at a glance

KILOMETER

0.0 From Nordic Center head onto Pancake Loop.

1.0 Turn left at intersection to continue on Pancake, or go straight on to other loops. Continue through intersection with Xmas Loop.

2.0 Return to start of Pancake.

Other trails on lower loops bend west-ward around ski area. Upper trails are reached by either taking chairlift up or climbing ski hill.

Boyne's Nordican Trails are among the state's best.

Boyne. Once you reach the top, there's a quick, eye-watering 100-foot drop to Vistas with a flat runout. Vistas travels all the way around the golf courses.

Once you're back at the start, you can take your pick as to how to get back to the base. Experts can tackle Koss' Crossing, a speedy little downhill tour that drops you nearly 500 feet over 4 kilometers. It will bring you back to the tail end of Little Hammer for the trip back to Twister. For a little mellower ride down, try Hilda's Hide-away, which runs right on the edge of the Disciples Ridge beginner downhill ski trails on a groomed summer road. It's rated more difficult (beginner downhill grade), and is a fast but gradual descent with no great surprises. Get back to the Nordic Center and you've gone about 15 kilometers. Expect it to take good skiers up to two hours to complete this route.

One more twist at the top. If you're used to most-difficult runs, here's one that will add another 5 kilometers to your tour. From Vistas Trail head off on The Grand Tour. Expect a series of eye-watering downhills and uphills, and because of those ups and downs, by the time you're back at the start you've probably covered about 1,000 vertical feet. Not too bad for us in the flatlands, eh? About halfway through, plan to stop at Vojin's Hut, named for Vojin Biac, a local Traverse City cross-country guru who helped design some of the initial trails here. He's also a former Czech Olympic team member. One drawback: The Grand Tour is not so hot on windy, raw days, because there's quite a bit of open area you must traverse along the bottom at one point. But if you've completed this and the rest of the trails here at Boyne, you'll have conquered just about the baddest stuff northern Michigan can dish out.

Camp Hayo-Went-Ha Trails
Camp Hayo-Went-Ha, Central Lake

Trail type ⚙ ▬▬

Location: 919 Northeast Torch Lake Drive, Central Lake, on the northwestern side of Torch Lake. From Traverse City head north of Elk Rapids on U.S. 31, turn east onto MI 88, then turn south onto Torch Lake Drive. The camp is about 7 miles south of the intersection on your right-hand side.

Also used by: Occasional winter hikers.

Distance: 16.7 miles over 15 trails.

Terrain: Flat routes combined with hilly sections up to 60 vertical feet, all set along Torch Lake or the woods across Torch Lake Drive. All trails are easily accessible.

Trail dificulty: Easiest to sections rated most difficult.

Surface quality: Single and double set tracks, depending on the location. Trails on the lakeside are groomed more often than those on the northern side of Torch Lake Drive. There also are some wilderness areas with ungroomed trails that allow you to break snow or try snowshoeing on your own.

Food and facilities: Ski and snowshoe rentals are available. Ski packages with skis and boots are $10.00 daily. Snowshoes run $5.00 daily. The trail pass fee is $7.00 per day for adults and students, and $15.00 for the family. Season passes are available, too. Complimentary coffee, hot chocolate, and small snacks in Kresge Lodge, where you'll also check in to use the trails. The Michigan YMCA runs the camp. Accommodations and restaurants are available in Bellaire on the southeastern side of the lake (see separate entry for Shanty Creek). In Charlevoix they include the Weathervane Terrace on the northern side of the channel connecting Lake Charlevoix with Lake Michigan, with 68 rooms, a pool, and a dining room. Lodging is also available at the camp by reservation. Call for information and prices; costs vary by group size. There's a hospital in Traverse City, 40 miles south, and one in Charlevoix to the north.

Phone numbers: Camp, (231) 544–5915; Web site, www.hayowentha.org. Shanty Creek, (231) 533–8621 or (800) 678–4111. Weathervane Terrace, (231) 547–9955. Charlevoix Area Convention and Visitors Bureau, (231) 547–2101 or (800) 367–8557.

WHO'D EVER thought you'd be returning to summer camp at your age to ski or snowshoe? But this is one of the most beautiful ski settings you'll find in the Lower Peninsula. All the trails are located on wooded grounds of this camp that's been in existence since the early 20th century.

They radiate from Kresge Lodge, named for the dime store and Kmart king who donated the money to put up some of the buildings at this 640-acre camp. He also was a camper here in 1916–17. The half-log-sided lodge sleeps 75 to 80 (individuals and groups) year-round. Many of the trails wander around camp buildings, but they also head across Torch Lake Drive into the dense hardwood- and evergreen-forested hills.

Upper Camp Trail is an easy one for beginners. It's 1.5 miles long and, from Kresge Lodge, follows the campground heading north. The more energetic in your party can stop at the fitness station across from the basketball courts to warm up with a few calisthenics.

Directions at a glance

MILE

0.0   From lodge turn left onto trail.

0.5   Turn left.

1.0   Turn left to travel back along lakefront.

1.5   Return to lodge.

Other trails start south of lodge and across road.

Go across the bridge and around the upper-camp cabins, which up to 200 kids call home during their four-week stays in warm weather.

Point Loop is short at 0.75 mile, but it's one of the favorites of frequent skiers. Views of the lake at the end can be breathtaking, especially at sunset or sunrise. Dress for the wind, however. It can be strong as it whips across the ice. Most skiers like to head out on the gradual portion of the trail that leads from the upper camp. It heads toward the beach, then parallels it before you turn left to the point. A cross at the point is a great spot to contemplate the beauty of what you see before you head back. At the lodge you can read the story of the cross in one of the pictures near the fireplace. Built in 1966, the 28-foot-tall cross is fashioned on dimensions mentioned in the Bible. From this point you can see the entire lake; it's one of the most majestic views on the entire lakefront. On the way back, there's a steep 20-foot drop just after the trail turns right, away from the lake, that beginners might want to walk down unless they're brave.

One of the more interesting out-and-back loops is Firetower Trail. This one generally has skier-set tracks and is ungroomed and very hilly in spots; you'll be climbing most of the way out. A 2-mile round trip will take you across the road from Kresge Lodge, where you'll climb about 200 feet to get to the old fire tower, built by the Civilian Con-

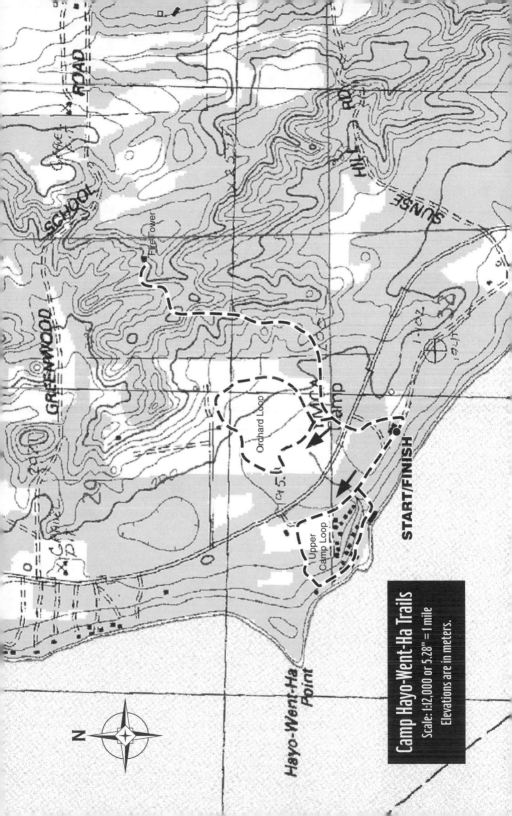

N

Fire Tower

Orchard Loop

Upper
Camp Loop

START/FINISH

Hayo-Went-Ha
Point

GREENWOOD

SCHOOL ROAD

SUNSE

HILL RD.

Camp Hayo-Went-Ha Trails

Scale: 1:12,000 or 5.28" = 1 mile

Elevations are in meters.

servation Corps in the 1930s and used periodically by locals to watch for blazes. It's pretty rickety, so *don't* climb it. You can relax on the downhill trip back. There are one or two hills up to 60 feet high that can be treacherous for novices and low intermediates, so approach them with care.

Another popular trail across the road is the 2-mile Orchard Loop. It's great for beginners and intermediates because it winds through mostly flat, open terrain that once—obviously—was an orchard. It's now the camp's Frisbee golf course, and you'll see the pins, or "baskets," every so often that mark the "greens." Ask for a Frisbee at the lodge and enjoy a game on skis for a few more calorie-burning stretches.

Snowshoers should obviously stay off the cross-country tracks, but you can enjoy the scenery just about anywhere through the property. Unless you're familiar with the area from skiing, stick with the grounds west of Torch Lake Road first. Since there are no snowshoe-ing trails, you'll be breaking your own unless you've asked at the rental office for advice.

Wilderness State Park Trails
Wilderness State Park, Mackinaw City

Trail type ━━━ ⬬

Note: If you plan to snowshoe, carry a compass or a GPS and know how to use it, or you could be in trouble if you're breaking trail. It may not look like much on the map, but take the park's name seriously.

Location: Carp Lake, 11 miles west of Mackinaw City, at the end of Gate Road. From I–75 take exit 337, Mackinaw City, and follow the signs westward. Take the first road to your left, which is Trail's End Road. It becomes Wilderness Park Drive.

Also used by: No one. Snowshoers can walk alongside the tracks.

Distance: 8 miles total.

Terrain: The park is a mixture of low bottomlands and some hills of no more than 60 vertical feet, but there are no steep inclines or descents. It is, however, extremely heavily wooded in most areas. Only 500 acres of the 8,500-acre park is developed, hence its name. The lack of challenging vertical is more than made up for by the heavy snows usually found here and the wilderness setting away from the park's developed areas.

Trail dificulty: Easiest to more difficult.

Surface quality: Groomed regularly and double track set.

Food and facilities: In summer Wilderness is a full-service state park, but in winter things move a little slower. The park's famous hike-in rustic cabins are available for rent, though. There's a hand pump at each cabin, along with a woodstove and firewood. You must bring your bedding or sleeping bags. They're booked pretty heavily through both winter and summer, so call ahead in plenty of time to reserve one. A rustic bunkhouse sleeps up to 24. Bathrooms are available in the park. Tundra Outfitters in Mackinaw City rents skis. There's a wide variety of accommodations available both in Mackinaw City on the Lower Peninsula side of the Mackinac Bridge and in St. Ignace on the Upper Peninsula side, though many close for the winter. Mackinaw City accommodations open all year include the Ramada Inn Convention Center, with 154 rooms, a heated indoor pool with whirlpool, and a restaurant.

Find others through the Mackinaw Area Tourist Bureau. The Mackinaw Trail use is free but a state park entry permit is required: $4.00 daily or $20.00 annually. Hospitals are found in Petoskey and Cheboygan.

Phone numbers: Wilderness State Park, (231) 436–5381. Ramada Inn, (231) 436–5535. Tundra Outfitters, (231) 436–5243. Mackinaw Area Tourist Bureau, (231) 436–5574; Web site, www. mackinawcity.com.

STOP HERE and you'll see why Michiganians consider themselves lucky. Wilderness is small yet huge, with more than 30 miles of coast that juts like a needle into Lake Michigan. You can still walk its beaches undisturbed in summer to either sunbathe or wade for the legendary bass action in the rocks of Waugoshance Point. In winter you can usually ski the trails unmolested by others as well, because you're in one of the most remote areas of the Lower Peninsula. Most trails leave from the campground area along Big Stone Bay.

Most skiers start out on Nebo Trail, a run of about 2 miles southward until it intersects with South Boundary Trail for about 1.5 miles, then head north onto Swamp Line Road for another 2 miles or so. It's a good workout for anyone and takes you into part of the park's interior and past a trailside day-use shelter and a rental cabin. At least you can see one to reserve for your next visit if they're taken and you're interested.

After parking at the trailhead lot, you'll go south through beautiful, heavily wooded old-growth pines and hardwoods that are so dense in many areas you probably won't want to do any exploring off the trail—you'd have to fight your way through to do so. A little way east is Mount Nebo and the trail's only hill, a 30- to 40-footer that's very steep with a gradual curve at the bottom. You might want to take off your skis on the way down in some parts.

From this point there are little rolling hills that run past Nebo Cabin and the trailside shelter. This shelter is a lean-to with a fireplace where you could build a blaze if needed to get warm, or if you've packed in picnic supplies.

Directions at a glance

MILE

0.0	From lot go east on trail.
0.8	Turn right.
1.7	Turn right, passing shelter.
2.0	Turn right onto Swamp Line Road.
4.5	Return to lot.

A short way past the shelter, the trail turns right onto South Boundary Trail. This is a fairly straight run with a few gentle slopes and nothing too hard to worry about. Turn north onto Swamp Line Road and you'll be pressing against the edge of a swamp. The trail bends and loops around following the edge and finally crosses Big Stone Creek, part of

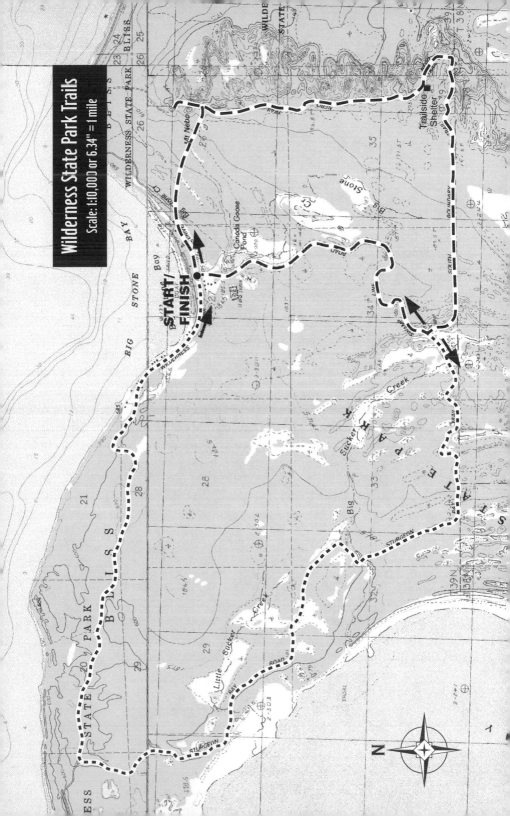

which you'll see later to your right as Goose Pond, formed when the creek was dammed here on its way to Lake Michigan.

Other trails in the park that you can try if you've got a bit more leg power include the length of Sturgeon Bay Trail. This 2.25-mile jaunt heads across two bridges on Big and Little Sucker Creeks into the western part of the park, along a portion of Sturgeon Bay, and past another wilderness cabin before turning north onto Sturgeon Bay Road, then east along the unplowed Park Drive back to the campground area. At one spot about 0.5 mile west of the Swamp Line Road intersection, Sturgeon Bay Trail intersects with part of Michigan's portion of the great North Country Trail, which stretches across much of the northern tier of states.

All along your journey you'll have the chance to see critters big and small, from deer and squirrels to grouse and even some wild turkeys and small winter birds. If you're the observant kind, as many skiers are, keep an eye out for coyotes, and trees bearing strange vertical marks. They've been left by passing black bears searching for nuts in fall.

Snowshoers can follow the same trails (take care not to step on the tracked portions of the route) or can go on any other trail that's designated at the park office. Just ask.

Heading off on your own through the woods is okay if you've got a great sense of direction, a compass, and some survival gear, but remember that it's easy to get lost in 8,500 acres of unfamiliar wilderness land—and doing so isn't very pleasant here in the winter.

Southeast Michigan

outheast Michigan's mostly flat or gently rolling countryside isn't the type of terrain most skiers think of first when they're looking for a great experience. But the region does have its advantages. For sheer proximity to the state's largest metropolitan area, this region can't be beat. Where else can the majority of the state's population drive an hour or less from their homes on a Saturday morning, get in a few quick runs, and be back in time to do chores around the house? Nowhere else. That's the region's biggest draw and the biggest reason to give it a try. The countryside most of the trails are set in is beautifully treed parkland, with all the conveniences close at hand and a few bumps thrown in here and there just for thrills. It's a great teaching area and a great location to bring kids out for an afternoon's fun in the snow. So don't sniff when your friends suggest trying out a few spots here. You'll be pleasantly surprised.

Maybury State Park Trails
Maybury State Park, Northville

Trail type: ▬▬ ◄

Note: Only skate skiing recommended on widest trails of the beginner's loops and the first half of the most-difficult loops.

Location: 20145 Beck Road, between Seven and Eight Mile Roads, Northville. From I–275 exit at Eight Mile Road and follow it through Northville's northern outskirts to the park entrance. The ski trails and concessions are near the parking lot.

Also used by: No one. Snowmobiles are prohibited in park.

Distance: 17 kilometers of trails.

Terrain: Mostly gentle hills, but two loops feature drops of up to 50 feet in elevation.

Trail difficulty: Easiest to most difficult.

Surface quality: Groomed regularly. Some trails in open areas are double tracked, but trails through the woods are single tracked.

Food and facilities: Trails are located inside an urban state park. Rentals and a small snack bar may be available at the trailhead; check with park rangers. Rental fees were undetermined at press time. Trail fees run $4.00 daily, or $20.00 for an annual park-use permit. There's a petting farm on the premises. Pit toilets are found at the trailhead and two other points along the trails. Water is available only at the parking lot. Restaurants in Northville include Guernsey Farms Dairy for inexpensive food from breakfast on, and Genitti's Hole in the Wall for a rollicking seven-course Italian dinner. Others are located downtown. Accommodations include the Embassy Suites Hotel, with 240 rooms and a restaurant. The demonstration farm is open for viewing in winter, but no programs are offered. Urgent care is available in Novi and several surrounding communities. There are hospitals in Livonia, West Bloomfield, and other communities.

Phone numbers: Maybury State Park, (248) 349–8390. Guernsey Farms Dairy, (248) 349–1466. Genitti's, (248) 349–0522. Embassy Suites, (313) 462–6000. Northville Chamber of Commerce, (248) 349–7640.

ONE OF THE MOST easily accessible cross-country ski trails for metro Detroiters is located inside this 1,000-acre park's gently rolling terrain, open meadows, and mature hardwood forest, as is a cast of winter wildlife from deer to birds. Maybury is on the site of a former state hospital. All signs of the facility were cleared away long before the park opened in 1975 as Michigan's first urban state park. There's a horse stable with rentals (except during December, January, and February) and numerous trails, including those open for cross-country striding and skating.

From the parking lot beginners can take a 2.5-kilometer trail that forms a gentle loop on a paved path through the predominantly maple and oak forest. Skaters can also share this trail on their way to the southeastern corner of the park. Beginners will cut generally westward on their one-way loop, which parallels the more difficult trail. Then, through a series of small easy hills and turns, you'll slowly curve to the right until meeting the most-difficult and more-difficult trails. These parallel the beginner run on separate paths until the easiest trail takes a sharp right and meanders back to the parking lot. From that intersection skiers tackling the 4-kilometer more-difficult loop can chart a course roughly southeastward on a tight loop that takes you to one of the park's three rain shelters.

Loop around and, while negotiating some 10- to 12-foot hills, head back to the intersection, where you'll continue left. This section is all on an unplowed, groomed road, so it's pretty open, but when it heads left you're back into the woods. Now you'll find trails for all three ability levels side by side for a time. The more-difficult trail arcs in a sweeping right-hander before straightening out and returning to the lot.

For the steeps, advanced skiers should turn a sharp left from the parking lot onto the most-difficult loop. Skaters can use the first half of this loop as well, because it's so wide. Watch for hills of up to 50 or 60 feet along mostly north–south sections of this trail. This loop will first take you deep into the woods and past the parks day shelter and the first of two ponds, a ten-acre marsh.

Here you can take an alternate out-and-back trail on the eastern edge of the pond to the headquarters road and pit toilets, or continue by turning right until you get to another rain shelter and the point farthest from the start. This is the park's hilliest portion, so expect some pretty precipitous drops—at least for Southeast Michigan—of 50 to 60 feet both approaching the shelter and moving away.

From here you'll be making a hairpin left turn up past the second, 2-acre pond. There's an alternate shortcut route here once you make a hard left that avoids another dogleg loop dipping south, then curling back north. At the next rain shelter and pit toilet, you'll be meeting up with your intermediate-class buddies for the ski back. About 1 kilometer later, you can either head back on the intermediate- or beginner-

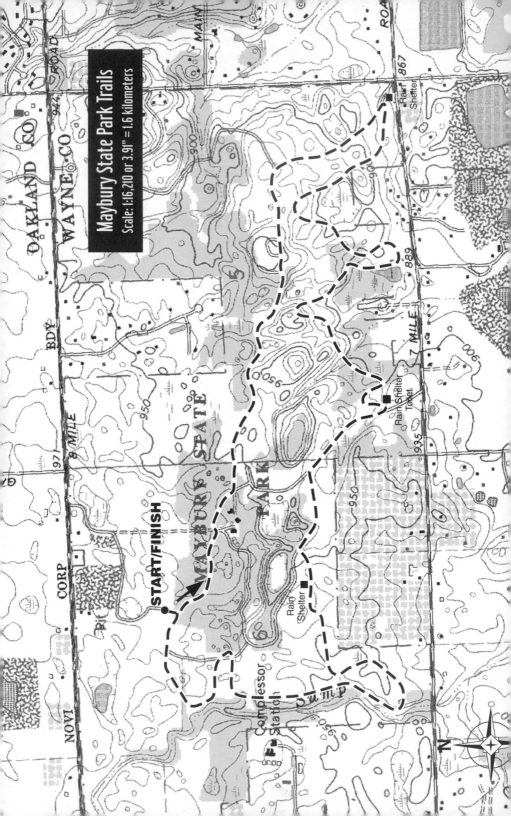

Maybury State Park Trails

Scale: 1:16,210 or 3.91" = 1.6 kilometers

START/FINISH

MAYBURY STATE PARK

Rain Shelter

Rain Shelter Toilet

Rain Shelter

Compressor Station

Swamp

DAKLAND CO

WAYNE CO

CORP

NOVI

ROAD

MAIN

8 MILE

7 MILE

N

level trail, or leave them again to continue on the most-difficult. This is another loop with some good hills along the edge of a creek valley running northward. Then you head for the finishing stretch past the group camping area—the only camping allowed at Maybury— and back to the parking lot.

Directions at a glance

KILOMETERS

0.0 Leave from trailhead.

1.0 Turn right at trail intersection or left for longer route.

1.1 Turn right at trail intersection.

2.5 Return to lot.

Afterward, take your kids or yourself over to the Maybury Living Farm, a replica turn-of-the-19th-century working farm typical of rural Wayne County. It's open 10:00 A.M. to 5:00 P.M. daily, with programs in summer.

A word about conditions: The past few winters haven't been very kind to Southeast Michigan skiers, either cross-country or downhill. Hefty snow dumps have not hung around too long. Call the park before you go to guarantee a good time.

Kensington Metropark Trails

Kensington Metropark, Milford

Trail type: ▬ ◄ ▩

Location: 2240 West Buno Road, Milford. From I–96 take the Kensington Road exit and go north to the park entrance, then head west to the ski center. There is parking available at three areas to access Trails A, B, and C. Skiing is prohibited in the nature study area and on nature trails and golf course greens.

Note: Skating trails parallel all three cross-country trails. Six miles of nature trails are open for snowshoeing in winter.

Also used by: No one. Nature trails may be used by the occasional winter hiker. A winter walking trail is also available apart from the ski trails.

Distance: Total, 8.3 miles. Trail A is 3 miles, B is 2.5, and C is 1.75.

Terrain: Rolling glacial moraine hills with drops of up to 200 feet on Trails C and B.

Trail difficulty: More difficult to most difficult.

Surface quality: Single track set trail and skating land groomed as conditions permit. Snowshoe trails are ungroomed. Trails are two-way.

Food and facilities: The ski center, located on the golf course, also offers rentals and instruction. Rentals are $6.50 weekends and holidays, $5.00 weekdays, with a small breakage insurance deposit, which is partially refunded when you return. A $3.00 weekend, $2.00 weekday, or $15.00 annual motor-vehicle permit is sold at the entrance. Snacks are available at the Farm Center food bar on Trail C. Due to challenging snow conditions in Southeast Michigan the last few years, always call ahead for conditions to ensure a great time. Accommodations in nearby Brighton, just west of the park at I–96 and U.S. 23, include a Holiday Inn Express at I–96 exit 145. It has 107 rooms and an indoor pool. Numerous restaurants are found near the hotel and more downtown. There's a hospital in Brighton.

Phone numbers: Ski center, (248) 685–9332, (248) 685–1561, or (800) 477–3178. Holiday Inn Express, (800) 465–4329. Livingston County Visitors Bureau, (517) 548–1795 or (800) 686–8474; Web site, www.htnews.com/lcvb.

PLANNERS FORESEEING the growth of recreation in the mid-20th century did things right when they proposed this beautiful park in western Oakland County. Set amid the Huron River Valley, Kent Lake, which is the heart of the facility, sits in a perfect glacial depression surrounded by hardwood hills. It's actually a dammed portion of the Huron River. Over the decades more amenities have been added, from sailboat rentals and great fishing to the golf course. And naturally, when cross-country became popular, why not (planners reasoned again) add Nordic skiing to the park? The result is three great trails all linked to form a network that runs parallel to the western shore of Kent Lake. The glacial moraine geology of the area makes for great hills of up to 200 feet in height.

A ski trip here also give families the opportunity to experience winter wildlife closer than you probably ever thought you could get to wild deer and other park residents.

From the southernmost point of the system, families can shake out the kinks on a small circular part of 3-mile-long Trail A, which loops the ski center. It's also a great beginner's area, but A itself is for folks who can handle more-difficult-rated trails, with rolling but not difficult hills.

Trail A mostly follows the snow-covered bicycle path to Maple Beach, one of two on the lake. It meanders right along the shore for some great views of the lake and some of the Canada geese that, unless the ice is too thick and the weather's too cold, make this their home nearly year-round.

Trail A's loop begins about a mile into your journey, where the route

Kensington Metropark trails are great for families.

Kensington Metropark Trails
Scale: 1:32,000 or 1.98" = 1 mile

N

START/FINISH

Nature
Center

Ice Rink
Snack Bar

Park
Headquarters

Wildwing
Lake

Golf Course

Picnic
Areas

Picnic
Areas

Picnic
Areas

Picnic
Areas

Picnic
Areas

Picnic
Area

Gravel
Pit

Gravel
Pit

Gravel
Pit

KENSINGTON LAKE

KENT

Trailer Park

SPILLWAY
ELEV 883

veers off to your right through old-growth oak. One out-and-back spur continues on down to Maple Beach and the ice rink, where there's also a snack bar. As you approach Maple Beach on this leg, be prepared for a good steep but straight downhill run of about 100 feet.

If you don't want to head to the beach, make a sharp left at the intersection and run through more of that beautiful oak grove in a loop that crosses two of the park's main roads—you may have to take off your skis to get across—then starts heading back to the ski center.

Trail B, also rated more-difficult, can be reached more directly by using the midpark ski parking area where Trail A crosses Highway 2. Push off through the woods until the next intersection, where Trail B users will turn right. Trail B heads through partly open country and abandoned hay fields, then makes a sharp turn to the west and then to the south. It's here where things get interesting—and fun. The trail hugs an old roadbed on this southerly stretch that makes a beautiful, slightly curving, 0.5 mile downhill run. On the eastern side of the route, look over at an abandoned apple orchard, while on the western side you'll see several huge maple trees that were in the front yards of farmers who worked the land before the park existed. After the downhill you're back on Trail A to the parking lot, or you can circle around and, if you're strong enough, head for Trail C.

This route is rated for advanced skiers and for many it's probably the least appealing because it's out in the open overlooking the northern part of the lake, and you'll be crossing roads three times. Still, you'll be rewarded with a couple of screamer hills with sharp turns that will either keep you on your toes or your face, depending on your skill.

You're tested right off on the "little" trail between Trail B and C, where you'll suddenly find yourself rocketing down a 200-foot-high hill adjacent to the park's toboggan runs. It's about a 0.25- to 0.3-mile run, but you'd better be an advanced intermediate to tackle this connector. That's your first challenge. The second is that Trail C generally has skier-set tracks only. If you take the right-hand run from where it joins the connector, the trail heads north in a loop, crossing first one road, then another near a bridge across the lake. It gradually gains a

Directions at a glance

MILE

0.0 From ski center head out onto Loop A.

1.0 Veer right, continuing on A.

1.0 Turn left at next intersection.

1.5 Turn left at next intersection.

2.75 Continue through intersection to return to center 7.5 miles away.

Other trails branch from Loop A.

little altitude as it loops westward, then finally heads into the finishing corkscrew, a steep, 75-foot-tall run near the park office that's an eye-opener as it curls around first left, then right. At the bottom you'll cross the roads twice more until you head back to climb up that little 20-foot connector or to the ski parking lot off Buno Road. There, look back on your ride down one of this part of the state's toughest runs.

I hope you'll have time between the hills to enjoy the wildlife, because nowhere else in the state will you be able to get as close to wild deer while skiing as you can here. Until the fall of 1999, Kensington was severely overpopulated with deer. While the population has been culled a bit, it's still possible to ski within a few feet of herds of whitetails; the animals are very much accustomed to human presence. Other wildlife in the park includes a large flock of Canada—don't say "Canadian"—geese, which are often found near the nature center along Trail A.

If you've still got the energy and have brought the sleds or toboggan with you, try out the runs in the hills on the park's western side, facing the lake.

Huron Meadows Metropark Trails
Huron Meadows Metropark, Brighton

Trail type: ▬▬◣

Location: 8765 Hammel Road. From U.S. 23 head west on Winans Lake Road to Wicket Road. Turn north and travel about 0.5 mile to Hammel Road, which heads northwest into the park. Turn north onto the park road to the ski center.

Also used by: No one.

Distance: Three major defined loops totaling 8.9 miles.

Terrain: Varies from open golf course fairways to moderate rolling hills no more than 50 feet high through woods in the park's southern half.

Trail difficulty: Easiest to most difficult.

Surface quality: Single track set. No skating trail. Trails are two-way.

Food and facilities: No ski rentals are available at the park. A motor-vehicle permit—$2.00 weekdays, $3.00 weekends, $15.00 annually—is required. Due to challenging snow conditions in Southeast Michigan the last few years, always call ahead for conditions to ensure a great time. Accommodations nearby in Brighton, just northwest of the park at I–96 and U.S. 23, include a Holiday Inn Express at I–96 exit 145. It has 107 rooms and an indoor pool. Also nearby in Whitmore Lake to the south along U.S. 23 is the Best Western, with 61 rooms and an indoor pool. Numerous restaurants are located in Brighton near the hotel with more downtown and near Whitmore Lake. There are hospitals in Brighton and south in Ann Arbor.

Phone numbers: Holiday Inn Express, (800) 465–4329. Whitmore Lake Best Western, (734) 449–2058. Livingston County Visitors Bureau, (517) 548–1795 or (800) 686–8474; Web site, www.htnews.com/lcvb. For trail conditions, call (800) 477–3191 or (800) 477–3193.

HURON MEADOWS is so precious to local cross-country skiers that few outside the surrounding area know about it, and that's the beauty of skiing there in this mini metropark. Most of the time you'll feel like you're out by yourself. Only one 0.5-mile section of the system is rated most difficult, so this is a perfect spot for skiing families out for a nice ride and experienced skiers looking for a bit of close-to-home exercise.

Trails on the northern side of the park cut through the park's golf course. All routes have markers corresponding to the easy-to-follow map, which also lists the distances between each to help you plan how long you want to ski.

From the ski center head out counterclockwise on the northernmost loop. It's a fairly open ski here, with mostly easy terrain as you head to the west then back south toward the center after a 0.7-mile warm-up.

Head immediately south on a second 1.2-mile leg around the western portion of Maltby Lake, where oak trees envelop you along part of the park's hiking trail. Just for diversion there's a 0.2-mile circle through the woods to extend this portion of the loop a bit. The trail continues on to marker 5. Here you've got a choice: Either circle around the eastern side of the lake for about a mile back to the center, or take off your skis and cross Hammel Road to the southern part of the system. Choose the route back to the center and you can also meet up with the southern part of the golf course, which holds another loop that's rated more difficult and, if you go the distance, will take you on a 2-mile trek through some enjoyable hilly glacial moraines that aren't so difficult they scare you off.

Directions at a glance

MILE

0.0   From ski center turn right onto northernmost loop.

1.3   Turn left at intersection to return to center or continue through to other loops.

If you cross the road, head to the right and meander comfortably on an easy trail that parallels the small road to the Cedar Ridge Picnic Area. Either continue to your right close to the Huron River the easy way, or jet down the park's steepest grade, a steep 0.5-mile ride that'll drop you about 20 feet, fortunately without any sharp turns to lay you flat. You'll rejoin your beginner friends at the bottom of the run. From here to where you started at Hammel Road, the trail is a friendly more-difficult route, mostly through abandoned farm fields that nature is taking over once again with shrubs and small trees.

Again, it's not the difficulty of the trails that will draw you here; it's the solitude and peace so close to one of the nation's largest metropolitan areas. Appreciate the park for these and you'll enjoy your visit.

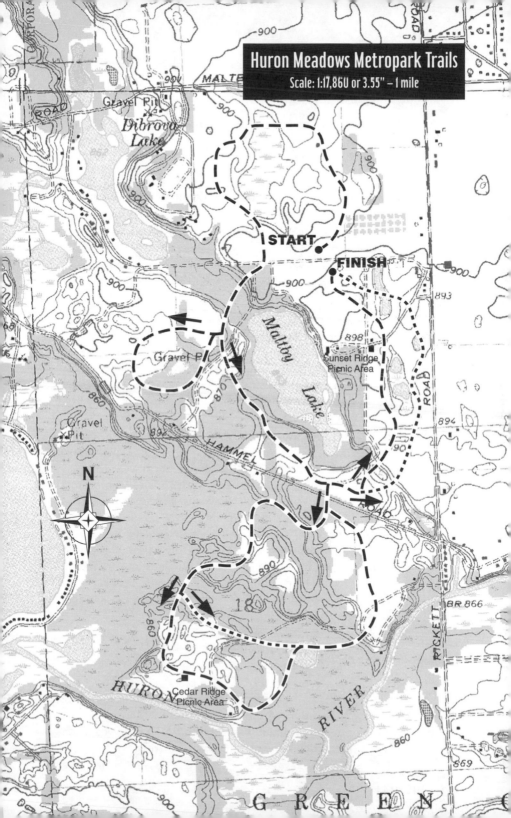

Huron Meadows Metropark Trails
Scale: 1:17,860 or 3.55" – 1 mile

START
FINISH

Stony Creek Metropark Trails

Stony Creek Metropark, Shelby Township

Trail type: ▬▬

Location: 4300 Main Park Road, Shelby Township. From MI 53 head west for 1.5 miles on 26 Mile Road to the park entrance. Go to the golf course.

Also used by: No one.

Distance: 12 miles of trails, most centered on the southwestern portion of the park.

Terrain: Trails in the western side of the park are very scenic, hilly, and wooded, with some routes taking in the golf course fairways. The elevation changes 200 feet from the lowest to the highest point, with the largest drops being 150 feet in two grades.

Trail difficulty: Easiest to five short sections rated most difficult.

Surface quality: Groomed when conditions permit with single and double track set trails, depending on the width of the trail. All carry two-way traffic unless noted. Trails are marked with orange-topped stakes or (in some locations) orange ribbons in trees. No skating is permitted, because trails aren't wide enough to support grooming.

Food and facilities: The ski center, which doubles as the golf clubhouse in summer, offers food service, depending on conditions. Ski rentals are available and cost $7.50 weekends, $6.00 weekdays for four hours. There is no trail fee. A park-use fee is paid per car load upon entry: $2.00 weekdays, $3.00 weekends, or $15.00 annually. Ski rental hours are 8:30 A.M. to 4:00 P.M. weekends and 10:00 A.M. to 4:00 P.M. weekdays. Rental skis must be back by 6:00 P.M. There are hospitals in Rochester 6 miles south and Clinton Township 8 miles east. Area restaurants include The Family Bobby in Rochester. Lodging includes the Red Roof Inn at Rochester Hills, with 111 rooms.

Phone numbers: Stony Creek Metropark, (810) 781–4242 or (800) 477–7756. The Family Bobby, (248) 656–0850. Red Roof Inn, (248) 853–6400.

BUILT PRIMARILY on the site of the former hunting estate of the Sheldon Family of Detroit, this edition of the Huron Clinton Metroparks is a beautiful addition to the recreational ski opportunities in Detroit's northern suburbs when snow conditions permit. Unfortunately, winter hasn't cooperated the last several years, making few skiable days available. But when there is enough snow, this is a great place to go because of its wide variety of terrain and the "up north" feel to the whole area.

The majority of trails weave through and around the hills of the golf course. Called the West Trails, they're named by letter. The West Trails traverse some interesting terrain; their loops are best skied when in combination, since they are all individually pretty short. Routes in the system's center are the hilliest. Bring your kids' sleds, too, because there are dedicated sledding hills throughout the park.

The most popular trail loop set starts at point A, at the northern end of the system, reached by the park's main access road. It's just north of the West Branch sledding hills. It's a generally easiest to more-difficult route, but it does take

A family enjoying the powder in front of the ski center.

in that hilly part of the park. Start by heading west on a nice, flat 0.3-mile stretch from A to B. Turn left to make a long uphill climb of about 100 feet to L. From L and following a right-hand turn to point I is a series of undulating hills that slowly drop down to I. The section from I north to J is short at 0.2 mile, but it's rated most difficult, and you'll drop a good 100 feet in that stretch. Beginners might want to walk down. From J north to C, you're once again in long, undulating hills. While this 0.6-mile stretch is still rated more- to most-difficult, compared to the drop you've just experienced, it's pretty mild through heavy stands of oaks, aspens, maples, and other hardwoods.

Turn left at C and continue, snaking along the park boundary through alternating heavily wooded and open areas. This is an easiest-rated 1.1-mile respite from your earlier travail past a cattail pond. Weave from D to E on another easiest-rated segment alongside Sheldon Road, consisting of small rolling hills through points E and F. At point G either duck south along another easiest route that borders Mead Road, or jog a bit north for a 0.3-mile more-difficult-rated series of undulations that take you to point K. You can either head from here to the ski center and the parking area, or go north up a 50-foot incline to get back into that hilliest middle region, and eventually back to A. The complete loop will take you around 90 minutes. Another interesting

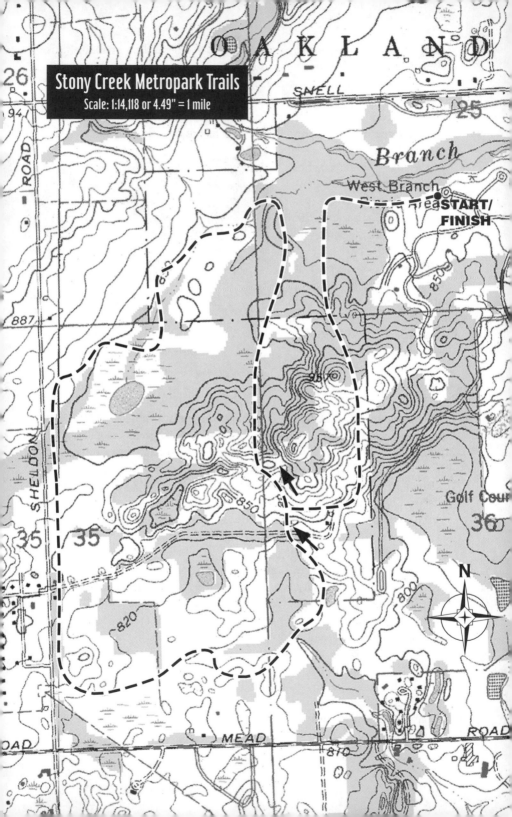

Stony Creek Metropark Trails
Scale: 1:14,118 or 4.49" = 1 mile

trail not marked on the map will take you up to the top of what's termed Mount Baldy, probably the highest point in Macomb County. That short trek heads up just east of point J; there's usually another trail that goes up on the other side near point L. The way down can be either steep or gradual, your choice.

Trails next to the ski center wander around the golf course. Aside from a couple of hills that earn two segments a more-difficult rating, these trails next to the fairways are all rated easiest.

The East Trails are not groomed and are for the individual skier who wishes to break trail. They traverse generally gentle rolling, wooded terrain through summer picnic grounds but are not nearly as pretty as the West Trail grouping. This part of the system totals 3 miles along the eastern side of Stony Creek Lake. There is only one real hill, between markers 4 and 5, a gradual drop of about 50 feet over 0.2 mile and a gradual climb of the same height from markers 7 to 5. Otherwise it's a flat but pretty run through the trees.

Those two great sledding hills are nearby. And don't forget to visit the park's nature center, open 10:00 A.M. to 5:00 P.M. weekends and 1:00 to 5:00 P.M. weekdays during winter. The center also has some snowshoe programs, including instructions on making your own. Call the center for more information. There also are special group rates for weekday use of the trails. This is a gem of a park well worth a ski.

Directions at a glance

MILE

0.0   From West Branch Picnic Area, leave marker A west toward marker B.

0.3   Arrive at B.

0.4   Arrive at C.

1.5   Go through D.

1.8   Go through E.

2.4   Turn right at F.

2.5   Veer left at G.

2.9   Turn left at K.

3.2   Go through I.

3.5   Go through J.

4.1   Return to C and turn right.

4.2   Go through B.

4.5   Return to A and lot.

East Michigan

This region of the state is diverse, but its lands have one thing in common: Except for the middle, which was once covered by pine forest, it has plenty of rolling hills that make for perfect cross-country. Snow conditions are best north of Saginaw Bay, and up to Mackinaw City, but during good snowy winters you'll be able to find great skiing in the south, too. Still, this section concentrates on places where the winters are cold, the snow is deep, and the skiing is great.

For-Mar Nature Preserve and Arboretum Trails

For-Mar Nature Preserve and Arboretum, Burton

Trail type: ▬▬

Location: 2142 North Genesee Road, 0.25 mile north of Davison Road, 1 mile from the Flint city limits.

Also used by: Walkers.

Distance: About 7 miles.

Terrain: Flat, with no thrill hills. You'll be traveling through climax-forest hardwoods, with four bridges to cross. Three go over Kearsley Creek, and the fourth over part of a pond.

Trail difficulty: Easiest. A minimum of 3 inches of snow on frozen ground is required.

Surface quality: Ungroomed, but usually skier set. Walkers are asked not to step on ski tracks.

Food and facilities: The preserve's visitors center is open 8:00 A.M. to 5:00 P.M., with rest rooms and water available indoors, but no snacks or rentals. The grounds are open 8:00 A.M. to sunset. Trail use is free. Center annual memberships start at $10, however. No ski rentals are available in the area. No dogs or alcohol allowed. There are plenty of places to stay in the Flint area, including the Holiday Inn Gateway Centre on the southwestern edge of the city, with 173 rooms, an indoor pool, and a restaurant. Places to eat in the area include Bill Knapp's, with three locations. There are hospitals in Flint.

Phone numbers: For-Mar Preserve, (810) 789–8567 or (810) 789–8568; Web site, www.formar.org. Holiday Inn Gateway Centre, (810) 232–5300. Bill Knapp's, (810) 239–4609, (810) 732–2240, or (810) 695–6722. Due to conditions the past several winters, it's wise to call ahead to check to ensure a great time. For information on the Flint area, including a listing of accommodations, restaurants, and other attractions, contact the Flint Area Convention and Visitors Bureau, (810) 232–8900 or (800) 253–5468; Web site, www.flint.org.

WHY SKI IN the shadow of one of Michigan's industrialized cities? Like Hillary and Everest, because it's there, and why not? You'll learn that you can have a great time even if you're not far away from your living room. There are lots of trails here that are fun, perfect for a quick after-work weekday trek or just a total change of pace. They are not second-class trails because of their geographic location. They should, in fact, be held in a special place in the minds of skiers, for if they're ignored, the entire body of trails of a state or region suffers. And that's the main reason why I've chosen to include a trail system like For-Mar.

The 383-acre nature area—once For-Mar Farms—was a gift from Forbes K. and Martha K. Merkley to Genesee County residents. It's now run by the county's Parks and Recreation Commission, to be kept in perpetuity as a nature preserve. The arboretum area is continually being broadened with tree plantings, and you're likely to see wildlife including deer and smaller ground animals. It's also a great birding area.

For skiers the most popular route is the deep woods trail. It goes across Kearsley Creek into the deepest woods of the park, through a mature forest of oak, sugar maple, and beech.

From the visitors center head east around Ground Water Pond, and then into the forest and across the footbridge across Kearsley Creek, which eventually flows into the Flint River. When the trail forms a Y, turn left (west) and you'll be headed right along the tree line with the creek on your left, then across an open field of what used to be a cattle pasture. Make a right and you'll be on Sugar Bush Trail, past an old river oxbow called Deep Woods Pond across mostly open land and then into a treed area, and along a fence made of old tree stumps put up by the former owners to keep their cows out of the area's low, swampy parts.

You'll cross those wetlands on a small footbridge, then turn left. Through this fairly flat, open country, you can step out and get moving eastward past strips of crops purposely left standing for wildlife, and a pheasant habitat area remaining for the wild pheasants that still inhabit the preserve. The trail loops past what's now a birding museum (open the first Sunday afternoon of each month from 1:30 to 4:30 P.M. in winter) and back around Runoff Pond. Once you're back at the tree line along Kearsley Creek, turn left;

Directions at a glance

MILE

0.0 From visitors center ski past pond toward creek.

0.3 Cross creek on bridge. Turn right.

0.7 Cross creek. Turn right to return to visitors center, or left to tour far eastern edge of preserve.

1.0 Return to visitors center.

Other trails fan out northward and eastward along creek and former farm prairie.

you're now going south. Stay on the stream's northern side to cross another auto bridge to Hawthorn Trail. You'll enter an area at the southeasternmost section of the park with a lot of second-growth shrubs like autumn olive, multiflora rose, and dogwood, along with a few major trees. It's a nice, flat, and very private section of trail that loops and

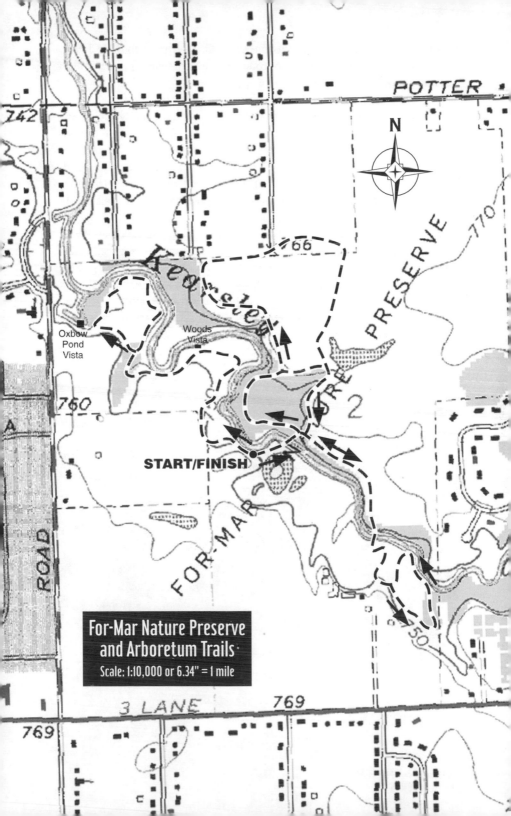

POTTER

N

Kearsley

766

PRESERVE

770

Oxbow
Pond
Vista

Woods
Vista

760

2

FOR-MAR

START/FINISH

750

ROAD

**For-Mar Nature Preserve
and Arboretum Trails**
Scale: 1:10,000 or 6.34" = 1 mile

3 LANE

769

769

742

meanders along the creek back to the start. Cross a road then go left to travel along a wetlands as you approach the visitors center and Ground Water Pond area.

To visit the northern end of the preserve, trek off to your left along Ground Water Pond Trail, which wanders in and out of the woods along the river's southern bank for some flat-out skiing along the tree line, or go across in front of the visitors center. Then, at the first Y, turn left and cross the river again. At the point where the trails converge on the southern side of the river, you can head off either along the trees or deep into the woods beside the river for a short distance on Succession Trail before reconnecting with the main route.

The trail continues northward on the southern side of the creek, along the woods line, then finally turns into it as the river makes a sharp turn north into the Young Woods. This is a young area, with a lot of small trees. Eventually you'll arrive at Oxbow Pond Vista, where you'll look down about 35 feet onto the old creekbed. Loop back along the same trail, or go south from the Oxbow Vista, then east, to pick up the route back to the visitors center.

When there's enough snow, For-Mar Nature Preserve has great skiing near a major Michigan city.

Corsair Trail Complex Trails

Corsair Trail Complex, Tawas City

Trail type: ▬▬

Location: 10 miles northeast of Tawas City/East Tawas off Monument Road. From U.S. 23 in Tawas City, turn west onto MI 55. Turn north onto Wilber Road about 2 miles to Monument Road, and veer left. Follow it approximately 6 miles to the complex.

Also used by: Parts of the general forest area are also used by snowmobiles, but they are confined to snowed-in national forest roads and, except for one overlook, stay away from skiers.

Distance: 35 miles of interconnecting looped trails on each side of Monument Road, and also connected by one trail crossing the highway. Trails are accessed by three plowed parking lots.

Terrain: Mostly low glacial hills with a few overlooks of 710 to 825 feet in elevation.

Trail difficulty: Easiest to most difficult.

Surface quality: Groomed and double track set, with a few hills suitable for telemarking (scout them first). Some backcountry skiing is available 4 miles to the north along the untracked Au Sable River Highbanks Trail. It's also great for snowshoeing and offers fantastic overlooks.

Food and facilities: There are outdoor rest rooms on site, as well as a log-cabin-style warming house at the Corsair parking lot on the complex's western side, near a creekside interpretive trail. Rental equipment and friendly instructions are available at Nordic Sports along U.S. 23 in East Tawas. Fees run $12.00 daily for adults, $6.00 for children under 5 feet. Lodging ranges from B&Bs, to some resort cottages that are open year-round, to hotels. Largest is the 103-room Tawas Bay Holiday Inn Resort, with an indoor pool and a bayfront restaurant in Tawas/East Tawas. Other facilities are available in Oscoda, 20 miles east on River Road Scenic Byway, about 4 miles north of the ski complex. Maps are available at the trailheads. Trails are marked with numbered wooden posts that correspond to the map. There's a hospital in East Tawas.

Phone numbers: For rental and condition information, Nordic Sports, (517) 362–2001; Web site, www.n-sport.com. Tawas Bay Holiday Inn Resort, (517) 362–8601. Tawas Area Chamber of Commerce, (517) 362–8643 or (800) 558–2927; Web site, www.tawas.com. Oscoda Area Convention and Visitors Bureau, (800) 235–4228; Web site, www.oscoda.com.

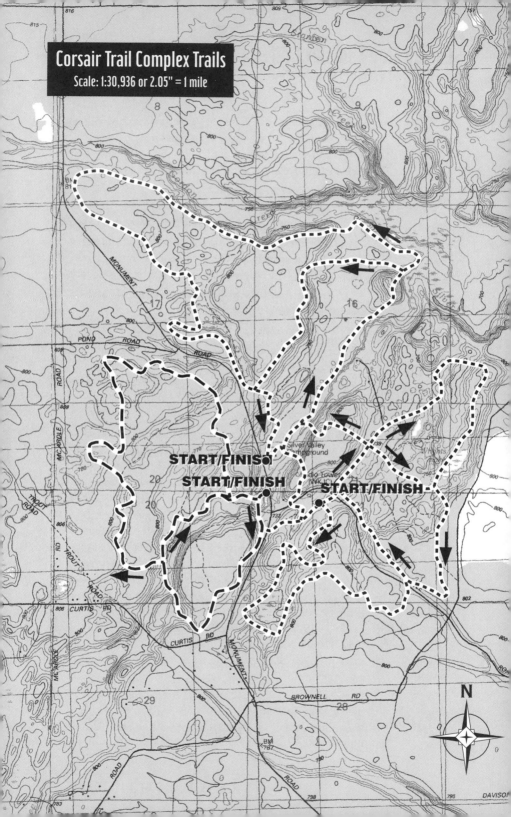

Corsair Trail Complex Trails
Scale: 1:30,936 or 2.05" = 1 mile

START/FINISH

START/FINISH

START/FINISH

Directions at a glance

MILE

0.0 From Corsair lot shelter (one of three parking areas), go left to cross Silver Creek.

0.2 Turn right at marker 14.

0.7 Continue through marker 15.

1.0 Turn right at marker 17.

1.2 Go straight at marker 18.

1.7 Veer right at marker 19.

2.0 Continue through marker 20 to return to lot.

Other trail loops start at Silver Valley Lot and Wright's Lake Lot, with extensive choices.

CORSAIR MAY NOT be the most challenging cross-country ski area in the state, but it's my favorite. Those wonderful warm, sunny days in late February and through March will often find us here gliding down a trail before heading into town for dinner.

Located in what's known as the Silver Valley area, Corsair was a downhill ski area and tracked toboggan run as late as the 1960s. Fears of hill erosion brought both of those operations to a close. After tearing down a large log lodge and replanting the ski hill, the area was redesignated cross-country, mostly at the urging and under the planning of Gary Nelkie of Nordic Sports. The word about the quality of its trails and grooming got out quickly, and Corsair is now one of East Michigan's

An overlook along the Au Sable River on High Banks Trail, near the Corsair trail system.

premier public Nordic ski destinations. On some days up to 1,000 skiers are out on the runs, but the trails are so well done that except for the parking lot, you'd never know it.

Trails on the eastern side of Monument Road head into the Huron-Manistee National Forest and meander through pine groves and meadows, with two outer loops also circling two small lakes. This side of the system is more conducive to skating. It contains some long expert trails that traverse beautiful rolling countryside. They're classified expert because of their length, since most of the hills here can be handled by intermediates as well. Another loop parallels smaller Gordon Creek to the north, where there are some great overlooks on the former downhill ski and toboggan site that's also frequented by the occasional snowmobile. The hill can be telemarked. On the western side of the road, routes are steeper. A few of the expert trails have sharp turns at the bottoms of hills, so be wary. Trails cross cold, clear Silver Creek twice on each side of Monument Road, so you can scout areas you'll want to return to in summer to fish for the creek's brook trout hiding among the alders and undercut banks (Michigan license required). Two recent additions include the log-cabin, gas-heated warming hut, and a short, marked interpretive riverside trail explaining how, among other things, the area served as a base for the depression-era Civilian Conservation Corps. The more recent Youth Conservation Corps members helped create the present trails.

Each segment between loops is from 0.4 to 1.5 miles long, so if the kids want to shorten their trip, that's always a choice. Benches also are provided at several spots. This is a very family-oriented complex, with skiers of all ages, dogs included, and some pulk sleds with which Mom and Dad can haul preskiers (no rentals, but special-order purchases are available through Nordic Sports).

It's a thoroughly delightful system. You won't be disappointed. If the parking's a bit too congested on your visit, drive about 4 miles north to the Au Sable Overlook and Lumberman's Monument, where on the 7-mile-long out-and-back Highbanks Trail you'll be treated to some of the most spectacular overviews in the state. Four power dams impound the Au Sable River, and you'll be on the steep overlooks where lumberjacks once rolled white pine logs to the water below. The forest seems to stretch on forever, and the bronze monument to Michigan's lumbering era makes for great photos. The trail is usually used enough to maintain a track, but the farther out you go, the less likely that is.

Mason Tract Pathway

Mason Wilderness Tract, Roscommon

Trail type: ▬▬▬ 🔳

Note: Snowshoers with a compass or GPS can explore the surrounding hardwood forest.

Location: 4 miles northeast of Roscommon on Chase Bridge Road. From I–75 take the MI 18 exit and turn north. Go through Roscommon and follow MI 18 about 2 miles outside town to Chase Bridge Road. Turn north. The trail begins just across the bridge over the South Branch of the Au Sable River. This out-and-back trail parallels the fabled South Branch through the Mason Wilderness Tract. Cars can be spotted at either end of the trail. A two-track road open in summer that parallels the trail is occasionally used by snowmobilers, but is far enough from the route that it poses no problem.

Also used by: The rare hunter.

Distance: 9.5 miles each way, with a 3-mile loop at Canoe Harbor State Forest Campground at the northern end.

Terrain: Mostly flat, with some low to moderate hills midway in near the high banks area.

Trail difficulty: Easiest to more difficult.

Surface quality: Single track, generally skier set.

Food and facilities: An outdoor toilet is available on the southern side of the river at the trail's southern end, and in the campground at the northern end. Food is available in Roscommon, 4 miles away, and in Grayling, about 12 miles west along MI 72 from Canoe Harbor, or via I–75 from Roscommon. There are plenty of accommodation choices in Grayling, including the 151-room Grayling Holiday Inn, with an indoor pool. There is a ski rental, repair, and sales shop behind it. Cross-Country Ski Headquarters is also not far from the trail (see separate entry). Instruction is available at both. No trailside camping is allowed. There's a hospital in Grayling.

Phone numbers: Grayling Holiday Inn, (517) 348–7611. Cross-country ski shop behind it, (517) 348–8558. Grayling Area Visitors Council, (800) 937–8837; Web site, www.grayling-mi.com.

GLIDE INTO THE DENSE cedar, pine, and hardwood forest trail starting at the edge of Chase Bridge Road and you've entered some of the wildest country in Lower Michigan. But don't worry, it's friendly wild. Donated

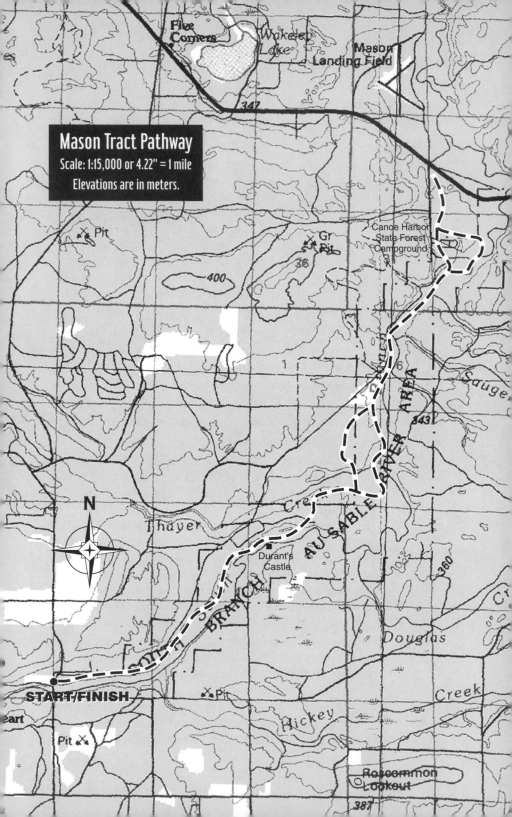

Mason Tract Pathway
Scale: 1:15,000 or 4.22" = 1 mile
Elevations are in meters.

Five Corners

Wakeley Lake

Mason Landing Field

347

Pit

Gr Pit

400

36

Canoe Harbor State Forest Campground

1

6

Sauge

343

N

Thayer

Creek

AU SABLE RIVER AREA

SOUTH BRANCH

360

Durant's Castle

Douglas

START/FINISH

Pit

eart

Pit

Hickey

Creek

Cr

Roscommon Lookout

387

to the state years ago by the widow of auto magnate George Mason, the tract officially takes in 16 miles of the trout-rich Au Sable River's South Branch.

A rustic wooden WELCOME sign alongside a two-track road sometimes used by snowmobiles just north of the trail entrance sets the mood for the silence you'll enjoy here. Relax and enjoy. The trail is state maintained in summer as a hiking path, and is single track set in winter for traditional skiers, although it may be wide enough to squeeze in an adventuresome skater alongside.

The mostly flat terrain is broken up about 2 miles in by slight hills, but beginners and intermediates will have no difficulty. Advanced skiers can come here not for the challenge of the terrain, but for its Walden-like setting. The pathway is rarely more than 100 feet from the riverbank. Kick off your skis at one of the signposts and walk over to enjoy the sights and the sounds of the river trickling against sheets of isinglass, amid tufts of falling snow. Beavers, deer, howling coyotes, and even an occasional bear wander the woods here. Here and there you'll see huge cedars drooping over the water, called "sweepers" by locals. Towering above the canopy, you'll also see a few ancient white pines that escaped the woodsman's crosscut saw in the late 19th century, when the region was in the heart of Michigan's lumber industry.

Summer brings out catch-and-release fly anglers after brown and brook trout. Points of interest along the route include the Mason Chapel, a wooden, nondenominational building looking over the river; the Castle, built in the early 20th century by General Motors pioneer William Durant, which burned to its foundation shortly after it was completed; Downey's, where you'll see the remains of a stone bridge foundation; Dogtown, named for the nearby sand hill that was used as temporary shelter for deer hunters' dogs when that method of hunting was legal in the early 1900s; and other spots designated by signs. The trail ends at Canoe Harbor, a state forest campground with rustic facilities that is open only in summer. Snowshoers can head off from the trail—but stick to the river's northern side, where you can follow the two-track out to main roads if you become disoriented. Carry a compass or GPS, because some of the undergrowth can be very thick. Walk or ski in and soak in the wildness.

Directions at a glance

Point to Point Trail runs east–west along northern side of Au Sable River's South Branch.

Cross-Country Ski Headquarters Trails
Cross-Country Ski Headquarters, Grayling

Trail type: ━━ ◄

Location: On County Road 100, 3 miles south of exit 244 or 3 miles west of I–75, exit 239 (County Road 103), then about 0.5 mile north on County Road 100.

Note: This is a privately maintained system of trails.

Also used by: No one but Nordic types, because this is a combination of state and private land.

Distance: Approximately 12 miles plus of trails over eight loops both behind the shop and across the street.

Terrain: Mostly flat, old-growth wooded land.

Trail difficulty: Easiest to more difficult.

Surface quality: Track set, all groomed for skaters.

Food and facilities: A facility pass costs $3.00 for adults, $1.00 for children ages 16 and under. Food is available at the sales and rental shop, and at the warming hut. Instruction is also available. Restaurants are available in nearby Roscommon and Grayling. Accommodations are found in Grayling to the north and Houghton Lake to the south. Rental equipment is available for all ages, including pulk sleds for transporting nonskiing youngsters; $12.00 for adults, $8.00 for kids 95 pounds and under for a full day. Rental fees include a facility pass. There's a hospital in Grayling.

Phone numbers: Call Cross-Country Ski Headquarters at (517) 821–6661; Web site: www.cross-country-ski.com. Grayling Area Visitors Council, (800) 937–8837; Web site: www.grayling-mi. com. Roscommon–Higgins Lake Chamber of Commerce, (517) 275–8760. Houghton Lake Area Chamber of Commerce, (517) 366–5644.

SET NEAR THE SHORE of Higgins Lake, one of Michigan's most beautiful inland lakes (once called the world's sixth most beautiful by *National Geographic*), veteran ski racer Bob Frye and his wife, Lynne, have fashioned this log store that has, over the years, gained a national reputation as a great place for advice, instruction, and a great day on the trails. That reputation has become even better.

Frye now tries to supplement Mother Nature and guarantee that his trails are snow covered every season with a snowmaking system spread from 1.2 miles to 2.5 miles of the trails he's cut since 1974, including 1.2 miles on one loop lighted by torches for weekend night touring. Snow will be made in a central spot and carted out to the trail to make this one of a handful of Nordic areas in the nation that offer guaranteed conditions. Frye plans to start making snow around November 1 each year to try to be the first in the state to offer skiing.

Walk your equipment across the street. The trail that first parallels the road quickly loses civilization to head into a deep hardwood stand. Choose from loops ranging from 0.75 to 3.25 miles long, all eventually curling back to the start. Trails go over small rolling hills and make great teaching sites; the Fryes use them to conduct their scheduled free clinics and private instruction. Trapper's Loop features a half-century-old reconstructed cabin about 0.6 mile in, where you can turn for the start or gird up for a 2-plus-mile loop that's ahead through more forest. Plans call for the cabin to be used as a warming hut, and the Fryes will expand their menu to sell food besides hot dogs on weekends. A bonfire is always going when there's good snow. But nothing in the entire system is so difficult that a novice with instruction or an advanced intermediate with good lungs and legs can't handle it. There are one or two hills that you may have to snowplow down.

Back at the lodge kick off your boots and warm up around the huge fieldstone fireplace, lounge on the sundeck if it's sunny, and enjoy some fresh-baked bread, homemade soups, and submarine sandwiches. Then browse for a new vest or hat in the ski shop that's one of the most complete around.

Snowshoeing is allowed next to the trails at Cross-Country Ski Headquarters.

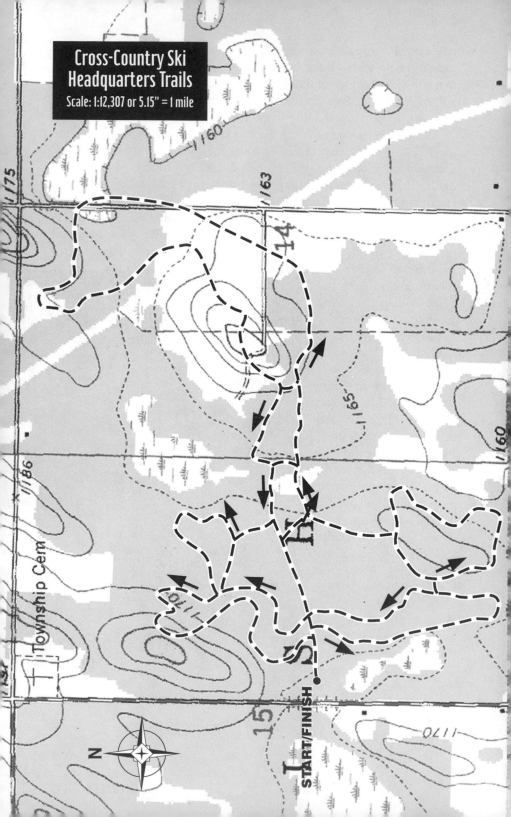

Cross-Country Ski Headquarters Trails

Scale: 1:12,307 or 5.15" = 1 mile

START/FINISH

Township Cem

N

Watch for the late-season sales as well as for specials in the Fryes' newsletter, published at the start of each season.

Cross-Country Ski Headquarters also is one of the state's 13-member Great Lakes Nordic Ski Council lodges participating in the annual Ski Fest learn-to-ski program in mid-January. And Ski Feast, an early-March weekend, sees resorts stocking trailside stops with cooks and chefs to serve up great food. The Fryes host a pig roast on the sundeck each year.

Don't forget to buy a jar or two of Bob Frye's Triple Black Diamond Bean Bomb spicy taco chip dip to rejuvenate with around the hot tub later. It's best heated and served with ready-to-drizzle melted cheese and chips, topped with great memories of a great ski day in northern Michigan.

Directions at a glance

MILE

0.0   From lodge head across County Road 100 into woods. Turn right, go straight, or turn left.

0.75 After turning right trail loops left. Go straight onto Wild Turkey.

1.9   Trail returns to start by turning right onto Partridge Alley.

2.6   Return to start by turning left toward road.

Hartwick Pines State Park Trails

Hartwick Pines State Park, Roscommon

Trail type: ━━━▶ .

Note: Snowshoeing is available on the grounds, but there are no marked, dedicated trails. Routes including Old Growth Forest Trail lend themselves to shoeing; just stay out of the ski tracks.

Location: The entrance is off MI 93, approximately 6 miles north of Grayling off I–75, exit 259. The park is open year-round, with skiing during daylight hours.

Also used by: Trails are tracked for skiers, but there are some foot trails wide enough to be used by snowshoers—in particular Old Growth Forest Trail, one of the park's most spectacular.

Distance: Trails total 18 miles, ranging from 3 to 8.5 miles.

Terrain: Depending on the trail, it ranges from mostly flat to rolling hills, with some large but manageable downhill drops. Rank beginners might want to walk down, but downhill runs are mostly straight.

Trail difficulty: Easiest to more difficult.

Surface quality: Dedicated cross-country trails are track set for traditional skiing and have enough room in most places for skaters. Footpaths that double as ski trails are skier set only. Snowshoers can use these as well.

Food and facilities: The trail fee consists of the park entrance fee, $4.00 daily or $20.00 annually. Park at the visitors center, where the tracked trailheads are located. Food is available at several restaurants in Grayling. Ski rentals are available behind the Holiday Inn, which also has a 0.8-mile, electrically lighted double track set trail in back, as well as 5 kilometers at an adjacent golf course. Both get an easiest rating. Restaurants include the Grayling Restaurant for great inexpensive breakfasts, or the Steakout Steakhouse on 1078 North Business I–75. Fuel up on great sandwiches, soups, and mulligatawny stew, washed down by great ice cream sundaes, old-fashioned phosphates, and malts in the 1950s-style Stevens Family Circle restaurant, 231 North Michigan in downtown Grayling. Places to stay include the 151-room Holiday Inn, with an indoor pool, hot tub, and restaurant. Other motels with varied amenities—from the basics to indoor pools to soak weary muscles—are also in town, along with B&Bs. No trailside camping is allowed, but a limited number of sites is open for winter camping in the park's campground. Electricity and hand pumps are available only along with vault toilets at $12.00 per night. The visitors center remains open, but the lumbering museum is open only in warm-weather months. There's a hospital in Grayling.

Phone numbers: Hartwick Pines State Park, (517) 348–7068. Grayling Holiday Inn, (517) 348–7611. Cross Country Ski shop behind it, (517) 348–8558. Stevens Family Circle, (517) 348–2111. Steakout Steakhouse, (517) 348–9811. Grayling Restaurant, (517) 348–2141. Grayling Area Visitors Council, (800) 937–8837; Web site, www.grayling-mi.com.

THIS BEAUTIFUL PARK is the result of the wish of a forward-thinking local lumberman's widow to leave a glimpse of the great forest that once covered northern Michigan to awe future generations. At more than 9,200 acres, it's the largest state park in the Lower Peninsula, including an 80-acre stand of virgin white pine and hemlock that makes for a peaceful, meditative ski experience.

My favorite trail is Au Sable River Footpath. This 3-mile loop starts at the edge of a dirt road off MI 93 and quickly engulfs skiers in the forest of hemlock, cedar, and hardwood. The trail is not track set, but skiers have usually gone before to make one. Watch for black specks on the snow. They're bugs nicknamed snow fleas, insects that pop out of the snow on sunny days. They won't bite. It's not long before you'll meander over the log bridge across the East Branch of the Au Sable River, cousin to its southerly Main and South Branches.

One trail at Hartwick Pines State Park takes skiers over a branch of the Au Sable River.

Hartwick Pines State Park Trails

Scale: 1:18,560 or 3.4" = 1 mile

START/FINISH
State Parks Central Warehouse

START/
FINISH Hartwick
Museum

East Branch Au Sable

River

Au Sable

Lumbermens Museum

S T A T E   P A R K

S T A T E

It's a beautiful brook that deserves a pause along its banks. Then you're back into the woods, past huge windfalls that look like they could harbor a hibernating bear or two, over the river again. One of the most magnificent parts of the trail is ahead, as you enter a huge stand of pine. The trail makes a hard left as it starts heading back. It's not a difficult route, but I challenge you to find a more enjoyable and restful 3 miles. Numbers on small posts that may be visible along the way correspond to a pocket guide that tells you what you're looking at. They're available at the visitors center.

The park's other trails, which double as mountain biking routes in summer, include three routes that are bisected by two shortcuts skiers can take if they tired or have children along. The 7.5-mile trail aptly named Weary Legs also is shared with a route from nearby Forbush Corner Ski Area (see separate entry). This route forms a large rectangle, practically encircling the park, edging close enough to I-75 at one point that you'll hear traffic, but not see it. The trip back to the trailhead includes a fairly hefty downhill. Once you crouch down enough to lower your gravity center, it's an exhilarating little run. The trail is rated more difficult because of it. If it intimidates you, take off your skis and walk down.

Directions at a glance

MILE

0.0   From lot go north onto Aspen Trail.

1.1   Turn left.

1.2   Turn left or continue straight on to outer loops.

1.9   Turn left shortly after crossing road.

3.0   Return to trailhead.

Snowshoers won't find any dedicated trails, but in the visitors center the past few winters, workshops have taken place on making your own snowshoes. Call the park for a schedule.

Snowshoers feel most comfortable on the park's Old Growth Forest Trail, which takes you into the heart of the virgin pines area. Trails also pass a replica lumber camp interpretive center that is open in summer. Let your imagination reach back a century to times when the sounds of lumberjacks' axes rang through the woods and oxen teams strained to pull sleds of logs and contraptions like the big red "Big Wheel" with its ancient log cargo slung underneath to the river and, later, narrow-gauge trains. Hartwick is one of Michigan's top parks. It's not difficult to ski or snowshoe, and the majesty of the place is breathtaking.

Forbush Corner Ski Area Trails

Forbush Corner Ski Area, Grayling

Trail type: ══ ◀

Note: Snowshoeing is available free across the road on the Michigan Shore to Shore Hiking Trail, for out-and-back trips. No pets are allowed on the trail.

Location: About 7 miles north of downtown Grayling in the tiny town of Frederic, just off I–75 at the Frederic/Lewiston exit (exit 264). Head east 0.25 mile, or, from Grayling, go north on Old U.S. 27 to Frederic. Turn east onto County Road 612 and go 0.25 mile past I–75. The area is usually closed Tuesday through Thursday.

Also used by: No one. Trails are on private or state parkland.

Distance: 37 kilometers, all open to both striders and skaters. Loops range from 1.5 kilometers to 11 kilometers.

Terrain: Heavily wooded, rolling hills, with some steep, twisty grades on most-difficult trails.

Trail difficulty: Easiest to most difficult.

Surface quality: Wonderful: among the best-maintained trails in the state. Single track set with skating trail groomed right beside. Grooming equipment is available for practically every snow condition to keep trails in great shape.

Food and facilities: Limited food is available at the main lodge on weekends. Brown-bag it on weekdays, or head for any of several restaurants in the tiny town of Frederic or in Grayling. Ski rentals are available. Trail fees run $15.00 daily, $38.00 per family. Rentals are $10.00 for classic, $15.00 for skating skis. Season passes are available as well, and if you visit more than eight times, they're worthwhile. Instruction is available with prior notice, and there's also a ski shop. Restaurants include the Grayling Restaurant for great inexpensive meals from breakfast to dinner, or the Steakout Steakhouse, 1078 North Business I–75. Fuel up on great sandwiches, soups, and mulligatawny stew, washed down by great ice cream sundaes, old-fashioned phosphates, and malts in the 1950s-style Stevens Family Circle restaurant, 231 North Michigan in downtown Grayling. Places to stay include the Holiday Inn, with 151 rooms and an indoor pool, hot tub, and restaurant. Other motels with varied amenities—from the basics to pools to soak weary muscles—are also in town, along with B&Bs. Forbush also offers a free lodging guide. There's a hospital in Grayling.

Phone numbers: Forbush Corner, (517) 348–5989; Web site, www.forbush-corner.com. Grayling Holiday Inn, (517) 348–7611. Steakout Steakhouse, (517) 348–9811. Grayling Restaurant, (517) 348–2141. Stevens Family Circle, (517) 348–2111. For a list of others, call the Grayling Area Visitors Council, (800) 937–8837; Web site, www.grayling-mi.com.

A CENTURY AGO, as logging denuded the land and the lumberjacks moved on, this tiny town turned to tourism and the tourists responded, staying here to fish the area's trout streams by the trainload. The trout may have survived the onslaught, but the town is quite a bit smaller than it was in its heyday. No matter to veterinarian and veteran amateur ski racer David Forbush, whose love of the sport is evident in his efforts designing, maintaining, and grooming one of the finest privately owned systems in the Midwest.

Forbush has expanded and maintained the trails for the last 17 years from his shop and warming area. Trails are wider than most, single track set, with skating lanes adjacent, perfect for friends preferring either. Forbush Corner, named for the centennial family farm his enterprise now crisscrosses, boasts the largest fleet of Nordic-only grooming equipment in the Midwest, ready for setting tracks in snow regardless of whether it's thigh-deep or only up to your toes.

It takes Forbush's crew about four hours to groom the system, and it's done regularly. Each loop eventually brings you back to the ski center. You'll head out through typical northern Michigan rolling hills through

Forbush Corner boasts some of the best maintained trails in the state.

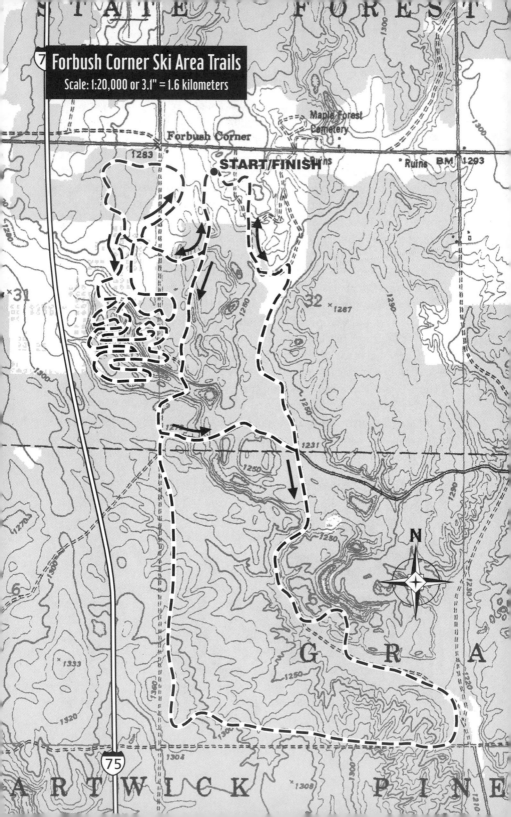

Forbush Corner Ski Area Trails

Scale: 1:20,000 or 3.1" = 1.6 kilometers

START/FINISH

pines and hardwoods, including some virgin white and red pines. The longest loop, the 11.5-kilometer Pines Loop, joins with trails in Hartwick Pines State Park for a while (see separate entry). If it's stormy, head for the 4-kilometer Back 40 Trail. It's a solid intermediate trail, a quiet respite tucked in a dense pine forest. The giants do a great job blocking the wind, and the sight of the snow falling amid the winds whispering through the interior is magical. On weekends Forbush often opens a rolling 1-kilometer trail for night skiing (check on availability). Advanced skiers can try the squiggly Roller Coaster Trail, and find out why it's called that when they tackle its series of hairpin downhill turns. Also, watch for interpretive signs in the woods at spots around the system. They provide some interesting reading about each trail.

One of the other great things about visiting here is the staff expertise. For several years Forbush has been fortunate enough to have racers and technicians both local and international on hand to provide tips on improving your technique, including New Zealand champion Craig Collins and Olympic team ski tuners. The staff conducts clinics throughout the season, so call ahead to find out what's up on your weekend up north.

Directions at a glance

KILOMETER

0.0 From lodge head onto trails linking to Pines Loop. Pass various intersections with other trails. Continue south on main trail.

4.0 Turn left at last intersection at southern side of Blue Loop.

4.5 Turn right onto Pines Loop.

9.0 Turn right onto top portion of Blue Loop.

9.5 Turn left onto trail.

11.5 Return to lodge.

The 9.5-kilometer West Trail system goes through the remaining portion of a 1,200-acre, late-19th-century orchard run by local lumber baron David Ward. At one time it was the second largest in the world, sending 11 boxcarloads of apples to New York every day in season. Ward planted it to keep his lumberjacks and draft animals busy in summer.

There are five optional routes, including Screamer, a downhill telemark run that goes nothing but down over a 50-foot vertical, and Lil' Stinker, a hefty uphill climb of 50 feet on a 35 percent grade, also considered advanced. You can bypass both by easier routes. And if at any time you're intimidated by a trail, Forbush says to take 'em off and walk—with consideration, of course, for other skiers.

Forbush also can provide lots of ideas for nonskiing adventures, from exploring the shops of Grayling and perhaps catching a glimpse of the elk herd to the north near Vanderbilt to a jaunt to see the ice formations of the Mackinac Straits at Mackinaw City. You won't be disappointed in this one.

Treetops Sylvan Resort Trails

Treetops Sylvan Resort, Gaylord

Trail type: ▬▬ ◀ ⬤

Location: East of downtown Gaylord on MI 32. Take exit 282 off I–75, head east through downtown, then turn north on Chester Road and east on Wilkinson into the resort complex. The Nordic Center is off the main entrance. Just follow the signs.

Also used by: No one.

Distance: More than 17.3 kilometers of trails.

Terrain: Mostly gentle, rolling terrain, with gradual elevation changes of up to 200 feet from the Nordic Center to the bottommost trail. Most-difficult trails, however, feature steep drops of up to 200 feet. The system also features two dedicated telemark areas separate from the downhill ski area. Most trails are two-way, but all of the steep descents are one-way so there's no worry about meeting others.

Trail difficulty: Easiest to most difficult.

Surface quality: Groomed regularly, generally single track set, with one side left for skaters. Because of their steepness, some runs are left ungroomed to help preserve the snow. All most-difficult descents are ungroomed.

Food and facilities: Treetops is a full-service downhill and cross-country ski resort in winter, and a golf resort in summer. The Nordic Center is probably one of the best equipped in the Midwest, with showers, changing rooms, and a carpeted locker room. Up the road, Treetops has 255 lodge rooms in addition to rental villas and a hilltop restaurant. Rentals are available at the resort's Nordic Center. Trail fees run $10.00 for adults, $8.00 for children ages 17 and under. Rental fees are $14.00 daily; snowshoe rentals cost $10.00 daily. Other accommodations include the Gaylord Super 8 Motel, off I–75 exit 282, with 82 rooms, an indoor pool, and free continental breakfast. Restaurants include the resort and in town, Albie's Pasties in the Wal-Mart shopping center for meat or veggie versions of this enclosed meat pie, an inexpensive northern Michigan favorite made famous by Upper Peninsula Cornish immigrants. Either take out or dine in. Downtown, the Sugar Bowl, with American and Greek dishes, serves breakfast through dinner and is one of the state's oldest family-run restaurants. The Big Buck Restaurant offers microbrewed beer and huge steaks. There's a hospital in Gaylord and a first-aid station at the base of the downhill slopes.

Phone numbers: Treetops Sylvan Resort, (517) 732–6711 or (800) 444–6711. Gaylord Convention and Tourism Bureau, (517) 732–6333 or (800) 345–8621. Super 8 Motel, (517) 732–5193. Albie's Pasties, (517) 732–8000. Sugar Bowl, (517) 732–5524. Big Buck, (517) 732–5781.

THE 1999-2000 ski season saw the resurgence of Treetops as one of the best places for cross-country skiing. Changes in the trail system the previous season or two brought groans of disappointment from those used to a network that had been called one of the finest in the Midwest. Trails had been moved north and made less challenging. But the complaints were heard and starting in winter 1999, an improved system incorporating many of the old trails was opened to bring Treetops back to the forefront of Michigan cross-country experiences.

Trails were named by the resort's Nordic director, James Richard, who's about as knowledgeable a skier as they come. He's made skiing fun here with play-on-word trail names that will keep you entertained—and, depending on how steep you like it, busy, too.

From the Nordic Center there's a great trail for advanced skiers to warm up on while beginners hone their skills. Kick-Off has some nice, subtle climbs and descents.

Beginners can kick

Heading out from the Nordic Center.

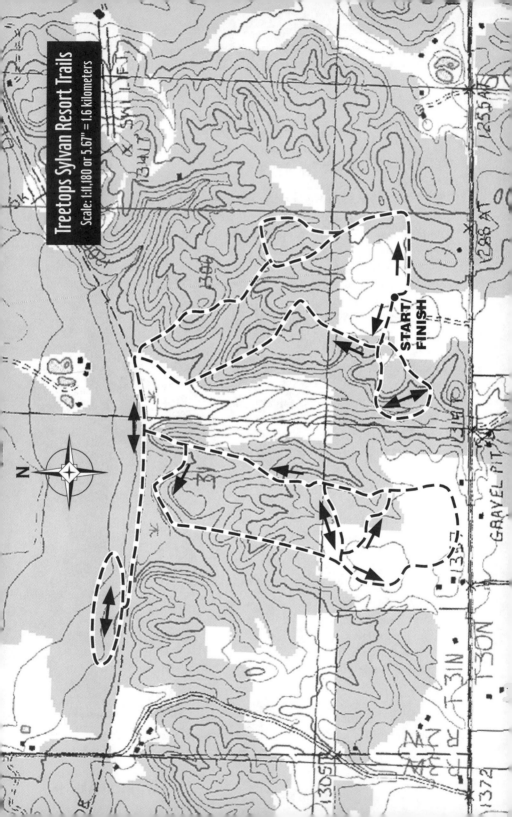

Treetops Sylvan Resort Trails
Scale: 1:11,180 or 5.67" = 1.6 kilometers

START/
FINISH

N

GRAVEL PIT

off on Kick-Off down a run renamed Tornado Alley, for good reason. A couple of years ago, a tornado swept down the hillside, following the trail and taking out virtually every large tree in its path. Most of the trees have been left where they fell allowing a close-up view of nature's power. Tornado Alley is a gentle 200-foot ride to the bottom of the hill and the Potato Railroad, a former railbed. Then you have a straight shot along the bottom of the valley, past two ponds named Bailey, and—for all lovers of *It's a Wonderful Life*—the George Bailey Bridge. Continue on Potato Railroad and you'll eventually get to Big Phlatt Circle, which is just that.

Directions at a glance

KILOMETER

0.0   From Nordic Center head out on Tornado Alley.

0.5   Bear right at intersection to continue on Tornado Alley.

1.5   Turn left onto Potato Railroad.

2.0   Turn left onto Highland Pass.

4.0   Turn right onto Potato Railroad.

4.5   Turn right onto Tornado Alley.

7.0   Return to Nordic Center.

If you're game, beginners can head back up via Tornado Alley, scoot east, and ride to the top on the three-person chairlift. Downhill runs also are open for telemarkers.

Intermediates might want to try setting off on Jacob Gnarley, which also is reachable directly from rooms at the Treetops Inn, one of the reasons this system is so popular.

There's a great view of the Pigeon River Valley from the top—one of several enthralling overlooks on the system. Then, if you're up to it, there's a great way down rated most difficult. Bloody L is groomed but not tracked. Telemarkers can drop off either trail and ski down between them for a great little 180-foot drop to Potato Railroad. It's one of three areas set aside for you.

If you've made it down to Potato Railroad, intermediate and advanced skiers can head up the uphill section of Highland Pass to Windy Ridge. Here, at 1,340 feet, you're at the highest elevation on the trails and some of the highest trail elevations in the Lower Peninsula. Everything is downhill.

Your choices for the descent include continuing on Highland for a long, sweet, gentle descent back to Potato Railroad, or playing rocket man and heading down a tricky shortcut called Blow Me Down, a most-difficult-rated ripper. The Plunge, another most-difficult trail, features a tight little drop of about 80 feet in a 50-foot length; you'll feel like you're going down a roller coaster.

Keep up your speed, because after the drop you're headed back up to Loose Ifer, another climb rewarded by a twisty-turny trip down. You'll start by zooming down a blind curve, hugging the fall line all the way around, until you drop onto Big Tree, a beginner's loop. It's definitely a challenge, especially on a good snow day.

The continuation of Loose Ifer is probably the most technical run on the system because of its quick, tight turns and rapid descent. Catch your breath and head back to the bottom on Big Tree, then up to the top on Tornado Alley. Combined with your run up Highland Pass, you've gone a good 10 kilometers

Backcountry skiers can take advantage of the thousands of acres in the neighboring Pigeon River State Forest. Hone your skills in a class, learn some great places to go, and graduate to become a "Treetops Nordic Warrior." Snowshoers can march off beside any of the cross-country runs, or join their backcountry skiing cousins for a trip into the woods they won't forget.

Wilderness Valley Trails
Wilderness Valley, Gaylord

Trail type: ━━ ＜ ⬭

Location: 7519 Mancelona Road (Otsego County Road 38), southwest of Gaylord. From I–75 take exit 270. Turn west until you reach Old U.S. 27. Go north to County Road 38 near Otsego Lake State Park. Turn west about 6 miles. The lodge is on the southern side of the road.

Also used by: No one.

Distance: 56 kilometers on seven loops from 1 kilometer to 18 kilometers in length.

Terrain: Flat to very hilly trails that travel through beautiful old-growth hardwood- and pine-forested country. Elevations from the lodge range from a high of 1,440 feet to a low of 1,300 feet, with vertical drops on the trails of up to 80 feet. The system features hills that are among the highest in the Lower Peninsula. Trails are kept as narrow as possible.

Trail difficulty: Easiest to most difficult.

Surface quality: Groomed and double track set. There are skating lanes on all trails where possible.

Food and facilities: A timber-frame pine lodge located across the street from the trails has rentals and rest rooms, along with full meals and snacks. You can also stay near the premises in private chalets starting at $125.00 per night. Other numerous accommodations are located in Grayling to the south or Gaylord to the north, both just off I–75. Many restaurants also are found in both towns. Trail fees are $7.00 daily, or $15.00 for a family pass. Night skiing only costs $5.00, or $11.00 for a family. Kiddie Corral Trail only is $1.00. Rentals are $15.00 daily for traditional skis, $18.00 for skating skis, or $6.00 for night skiing; the fees include a trail pass. Pulks rent for $10.00 daily. Open 9:00 A.M. to 5 :00 P.M. weekends, and open daily through the Christmas and New Year's holidays. There's a hospital in Gaylord.

Phone numbers: Call Wilderness Valley at (231) 585–7090. Gaylord Convention and Tourism Bureau, (517) 732–4000 or (800) 345–8621; Web site, www.gaylord-mich.com.

YOU CAN THANK the glaciers that once spread over most of Michigan for this ski area, nestled in the high hardwood hills southwest of Gaylord. This four-season complex—golf in spring, summer, and fall—is in the

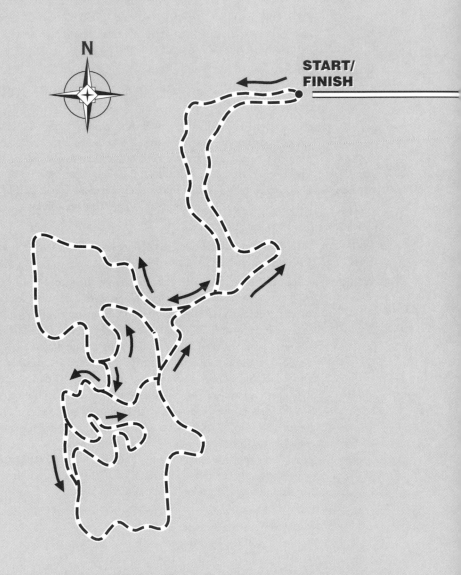

Wilderness Valley Trails
No scale map available for this trail

GOLF
COURSE

N

START/
FINISH

heart of Otsego County's snowbelt. Because of its high ridges, the area often gets dumped on while people a few miles away are seeing only a dusting. It's a great system that starts out easy and gets progressively more difficult the farther out you go, so depending on how hard you want to work, you can either stretch your visit or make it brief.

The ski trails are set over more than 1,200 acres of woodsy ridges. From the lodge you'll first head west on a series of two easiest-rated loops. The first, a 1 kilometer, starts off in open country over the center's practice putting green with gentle rolls so you can maintain a nice pace for the first 0.8 kilometer. It's also picturesque, because it travels around a small lake.

The next loop turns to the south, so you'll see more of the local terrain. It still features lots of gently rolling downhills, though, especially on the way back. The first hill, Brew's Boogie, is a gentle downhill. There's an extremely gradual climb up to Paige's Path, and a nice descent into Pine Valley on the return leg to the lodge.

Once you hit the more-difficult trails, the country becomes much more secluded. Intermediate and advanced skiers will break right away from the second easy loop and go through a small tunnel to get to their kind of trails. The route then turns to your right to climb a nice, steep hill. You might want to herringbone up to the top. In the area called Shaw's Snake, you'll be on the crest of a dense hardwood forest ridge that the trail wiggles through, in some areas fairly narrowly. Found just before a turn to the left is the first good steep pitch—a scary drop spread over 200 yards of trail. You'll be rewarded a few strides later with a chance to head onto Lookout Point for a spectacular view of the Mackinaw State Forest that cuts away 200 feet below you. Look hard and you'll see the headwaters of the Manistee River in the valley.

Now you'll keep heading south into steeper, rolling terrain. The next hill is Herrick's, named for the man who secured the annual Michigan Cup ski race for the area.

Directions at a glance

KILOMETER

0.0 From lodge head west onto first loop.

1.0 Turn left from Brew's Boogie onto Paige's Path.

2.0 Return to first loop.

2.5 Return to lodge.

Other trails head off to your right from Brew's-Paige's intersection.

It takes place in mid-February. Intermediate and advanced skiers have a decision to make here: The more-difficult loop turns right, while those wanting a real thrill can head left down Champagne Chute. You first have to climb some pretty steep stuff on Ridge Run. You'll be at the system's

Overnight camping is popular on several northern trails, either in tents or cabins at campgrounds.

highest point at 1,440 feet when you arrive at the top. Groomers have added a gentle ess turn into the trail to make a gradual arc that should help you slow things down a bit. You won't have to snowplow, but be ready for speeds of up to 30 miles an hour over this 80-foot vertical drop spread over 0.8 kilometer of trail.

The chute winds around and touches the intermediate trails again back in a valley, through some nice hardwoods. Expert skiers can soon head left again onto the Whoop-De-Dos—a series of four steep downhill glides perhaps 200 feet long each—followed by uphills and flats. You can generally carry enough speed from the downhill leg to head up without any herringboning or poling. Intermediates, meanwhile, have a nice gradual drop down to the spot where they meet up again with their friends at the end of Whoop-De-Dos.

The loop then heads down into ponderosa, an open area that leads into a section of mature pines on a gradual uphill slope but with plenty of downhills mixed in. Just past the 8-kilometer mark, the route drops over what in summer is the 15th tee in stair-step fashion. Then you'll head back into the hardwoods on your way back to the tunnel.

Garland Resort Trails
Garland Resort, Lewiston

Trail type: ▬ ◄ ⬮

Location: Just outside Lewiston on County Road 489. There are a couple of ways to get there. You can leave I–75 at Gaylord and head east on MI 32, then go south on 489 for about 9 miles. You can also exit I–75 at Grayling, drive east on MI 72 until the tiny hamlet of Luzerne, then head north on County Road 489 for 12 miles until you see the welcome glow of lights announcing the resort complex.

Also used by: The occasional deer or elk, and evening sleigh rides (see description).

Distance: 40 kilometers of trails leave from the main lodge.

Terrain: Trails run alongside Garland's golf course and head into the oak and pine forest. Snowmobile rentals and packages are available, but you aren't allowed to snowmobile on the resort property; those trails are adjacent. There's also 5 kilometers of snowshoe trails leaving from near the main lodge and snowshoe rental

Trail difficulty: Easiest to more difficult.

Surface quality: Groomed regularly with one to two tracks, depending on location.

Food and facilities: Garland Resort is one of the state's outstanding properties. A weekend here is a must at least once. No trail fees for resort guests here on a ski package; others pay $10.00 daily. Garland's renowned Gourmet Glides are $47.00 for nonguests, around $140.00 for packages that combine one night's lodging and the Glide. Early-season midweek ski packages with dining start at around $90.00 per person, double occupancy. Rentals start at $15.00 for adults, $8.00 for children. Children's sizes and instruction are available. Snowshoe rentals cost $5.00 per hour or $15.00 per day. Other spots in the area include the charming Lakeview Hills Inn B&B, with its own set of trails. Restaurants include the Redwood Motor Inn. Next door is the Redwood Steak House, open for dinner only. Other places to stay are found in Gaylord and Grayling. There are hospitals in Gaylord and Grayling.

Phone numbers: Redwood Motor Inn, (517) 786–2226. Lakeview Hills, (517) 786–3445. Garland Resort, (517) 786–2211 or (800) 968–0042; Web site, www.garlandusa.com. Lewiston Area Chamber of Commerce, (517) 786–2293 (can be hard to get hold of).

TURN INTO THE beautifully lighted entrance and you'll think you've entered cross-country heaven. What Garland lacks in trail difficulty, it makes up for in everything else. Start with the lodge: It's the largest log structure east of the Mississippi and the state's only resort facility given a four-diamond rating by the AAA.

Step through the huge doors into the lobby and in front of you is Garland's signature restaurant, Herman's. You'll know instantly that what you paid to get a room here was money wisely spent. The rooms themselves are just as spectacular. If possible, get an upper-floor room looking over the course. You'll find deep carpeting to soothe your feet after a day on the trail; four-poster beds adorn some rooms, along with gas fireplaces. Family rooms on the lower floor with two beds and a sleeper sofa are just as pleasant. Herman's is expensive—and worth it. Great breakfasts, too. Take back some preserves made on the premises by one of its chefs, Shelly.

Trails meander along the edges of Garland's golf courses and are not difficult. A great ski shop at one end of the main lodge can outfit everyone with rental equipment, or can set you up with your own. Glide down a short incline and you're off. Snowshoers can also try one of the state's few routes dedicated just to them. All are single tracked. There's 5 kilometers of trails winding off Carousel and Persnickety Ski Trails near the main lodge before heading into the woods. The trails are groomed with snowshoes, so if there's a heavy snow, chances are Garland personnel have been or will be out packing them down.

Start with Aspen Alley, a 1.8-kilometer two-way route that connects with the others along a heavily wooded path. The first off it is Squirrel Avenue, a 0.5-kilometer shorty that's close enough to the lodge for guests who just want to try a taste of snowshoeing before heading in again. The rest sport a variety of terrain. The hilliest route is Rattlesnake Ridge. Its 1.6 kilometers parallels the area's most difficult ski trail, and you'll go up and down hills from 30 to 40 feet in elevation. Black Bear is farthest from the lodge. Although it's 1.2 kilometers long, it's rated more difficult because you've got to tread nearly 2 kilometers to get to it. They're all heavily wooded. An inset on the ski trail map shows their location.

If you're here during a Gourmet Glide weekend (select weekends from January through mid-March), you've just got to participate. It's a great

> ## Directions at a glance
>
> KILOMETER
>
> 0.0   From ski center head past lodge.
>
> 2.6   Turn left for circle route back to start.
>
> 5.0   Return to lodge.
>
> *Other routes take you deeper into the Garland property, especially on Gourmet Glide (see story).*

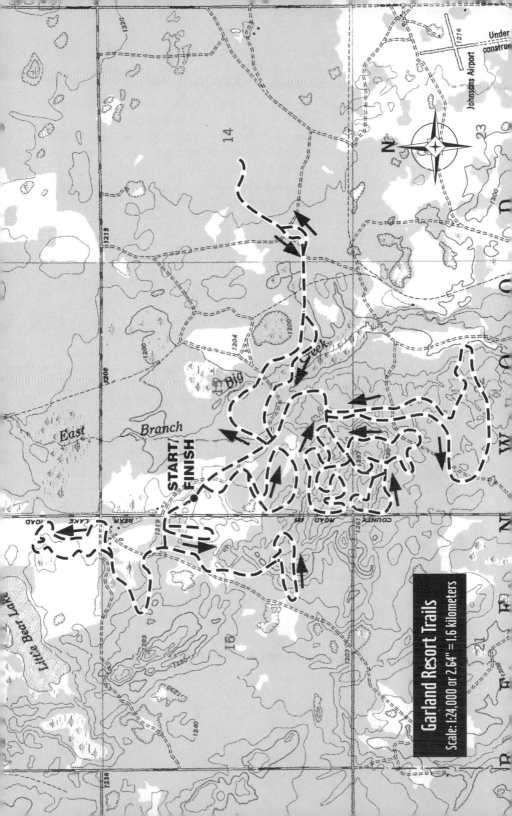

Garland Resort Trails
Scale: 1:24,000 or 2.64" = 1.6 kilometers

experience for the whole family. Here's a preview: The Glide usually runs on Carousel, Rainbow, Fat Free, and Buckhorn Trails. This route takes you in a big loop from the shadow of the log main lodge, along one of Garland's golf courses, past a lake, and eventually through pine forest. After skiing next to the golf course, your first stop is the ninth-hole refreshment stand for a taste of dishes that might include fettuccine Alfredo, wild game sausage, or fruit fondue. But don't overdo it; this is just one of five food stations, the first being breakfast in the lodge lounge.

After about 3 kilometers through the woods along a snowy road and through a tall fence that guards the resort's Garland Safari elk, trophy deer, and boar herd (hunts are available; you won't see the aggressive boars because they and stretch pants and gaiters don't mix), you'll come to owner Ron Otto's hunting cabin, Buckhorn.

Surrounded by trophies from past hunts, you'll sample more treats—perhaps carved wild game—before it's time to turn around. The next stop is a small pond where, if you're lucky, you can catch trout to be cooked on the spot or, like most folks, just partake of what's already fried up. Back at the lodge, pad down the hallway to the conference center wing and enjoy dessert. Then head over to the hot tub (if there's room) or lower-level pool to relax after the 10-kilometer jaunt you've just made. Depending on snow depths, the route will change, but the stops won't.

Buckhorn Lodge also is the setting for Garland's unique Zhivago Night dinners offered most winter weekends. After a 20-minute sleigh ride, walk

into Buckhorn to greet the Hanafords, a husband-and-wife duo playing "Lara's Theme" from *Doctor Zhivago,* and prepare to be dazzled with a five-course dinner. The evening features items like veal and morel terrine, grilled scallion polenta with mushrooms, venison, and decadent desserts, accompanied by at least two types of wine and after-dinner drinks before you're jingled back in the sleigh to the main lodge. Again, at around $350.00 per couple, per night, it's expensive, but with someone special, it's a magical experience you'll remember for a lifetime.

Trails start from Garland's beautiful main lodge.

Thunder Bay Resort Trails

Thunder Bay Resort, Hillman

Trail type: ▬ ◄ ▦

Location: 27800 MI 32 East in Hillman, approximately 22 miles west of Alpena. Thunder Bay, named for the river that meanders behind the lodge complex, is a golf resort in summer and offers skiing and elk viewing in winter.

Also used by: Local deer. Trails are on private land.

Distance: 3 miles of trails on the premises, with other state forest trails nearby (see the separate entry for Norway Ridge Pathway). More than 1.5 miles of trails on the Thunder Bay River's northern side are suitable for snowshoers, with the possibility of seeing elk.

Terrain: Mostly flat to rolling, with one exception.

Trail difficulty: Easiest to most difficult. Groomed, double track set, with skating lanes on the resort's golf course.

Surface quality: Groomed regularly as needed; double track set and skating lanes on all trails.

Food and facilities: Fees run $6.00 daily and $60.00 per season; family season pass is $120. Rest rooms are available along the eastern-side ski trail route. Thunder Bay Resort offers luxury condo lodging in villas and log-cabin chalets. Each unit sleeps from 2 to 12 for a total of up to 148, with a centralized outdoor hot tub. Units can be split into smaller rooms or made up for large groups. Many have full kitchens. You'll also find on the premises a lounge and a restaurant serving breakfast through dinner. Many guests also sign up for the gourmet sleigh ride dinner package. Rentals, including 20 sets of children's equipment, run about $12.00 a day, $20.00 per weekend for classic skis; $15.00 daily, $25.00 for the weekend for skating skis. No instruction is available. Weekend package stays cost from $159.00 to $213.00, depending on the lodging. Packages also include two nights' lodging, two breakfasts, and two to three day passes for skiing or snowshoeing and other activities. Less expensive weekday packages are also available. Other places to stay and more restaurants are found in Alpena. There's a hospital in Alpena.

Phone numbers: Thunder Bay Resort, (800) 729–9375; Web site, www.thunderbaygolf.com. Hillman Chamber of Commerce, (517) 742–3739. Alpena Convention and Visitors Bureau, (517) 354–4181 or (800) 425–7362.

THE SMALL HAMLET of Hillman is hardly the setting you'd expect for a resort with so much to offer, but here it is just the same. Located on the northern side of MI 32, Thunder Bay Resort has undergone a tidy expansion under owner Jack Matthias. The cozy restaurant on the lower level also serves as the spot where renters can pick up their equipment and head outside to the trails. They are bisected by Country Club Drive, the road that heads back toward the Thunder Bay River and the snowshoeing area. Loops are purposely short so if you're an exhausted beginner, you can head back to your room early.

All the trails here are marked with color-coded diamonds (blue, brown, green, yellow, and red) to help you on your way; none is difficult. Start from the lodge and take the Blue Trail on the western side of Country Club Road. You'll be in mostly rolling, open country here, meandering along the resort's golf course. Stay on the Blue Trail back to the start and you'll have gone about 3 miles. The route is pretty

> ## Directions at a glance
>
> MILE
>
> 0.0   From main lodge complex go north.
>
> 0.5   Turn right.
>
> *From here, trails meander in 0.5-mile lengths north and south over golf course. Skiers can return to lodge at any time by heading west, or following trail's entire length.*

easy except for the far northern end, which earns its most-difficult rating in spades. It scoots over a 140-foot elevation change downhill past a trout pond, crosses a road, and ducks in and out of the trees until it rejoins the Green Trail. Take a left on the Green Trail or go right through the trees on the Blue. It rejoins the Green in a bit, and then heads off again to the right for another, even closer look at the river and woods. Keep following the Blue or head off on one of the short byways. Either way you'll climb a nearly 100-foot hill up from the valley before you're back on the course. All trails will take you back to the lodge. The Blue Trail on the western course is probably the prettiest route because of its proximity to the river, but it's obviously the most challenging.

On the other side, the color codes are repeated. Take the Yellow Trail due north past the villas and communal outdoor hot tub gazebo and you'll be nearing the river after about 0.5 mile. River access is blocked on this side by a road, but you'll enjoy some of Thunder Bay Resort's most heavily wooded routes, protected from the winds that sweep the more open western side. Rest rooms are on the far eastern reach of the Blue Trail East. The trail then doglegs back and forth in nearly 0.5-mile segments until you've got the opportunity to call it quits and take a shortcut back to the lodge if you don't have the energy to zigzag up and back the rest of the course.

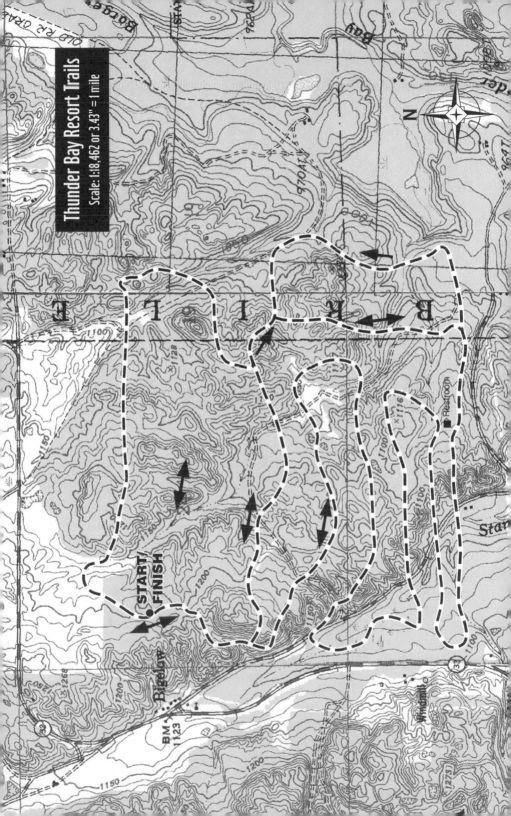

See Thunder Bay Resort's private elk herd on a snowshoe hike or a dinner sleigh ride.

Snowshoers can head directly up Country Club Drive and across the river via a bridge to 1.5 miles of wide hiking and sleigh trails that double as their routes in winter. A Michigan Rails to Trails project turned an old railroad grade into a state-owned snowmobile route running from Alpena to Hillman. It's a few yards from the snowshoe trail, but except for busy weekends, traffic should be light. The snowshoe trail follows a good portion of the river, but you can cross the snowmobile trail and sidle up to the fence for a possible glimpse of some of the resort's elk. This area is heavily covered in hardwoods and a beautiful stand of hemlocks. Some of it is primeval stuff. It's best to stay on the marked routes.

If you want to see more, sign up for the resort's wonderful treat, a combination elk viewing and gourmet sleigh ride dinner. Starting from the lodge, the sleigh carries you toward the snowshoe routes over the Thunder Bay River to view these huge, magnificent creatures. The trip used to include a bus ride west of Hillman before the sleigh ride to view part of Michigan's wild herd—now numbering more than 1,000. But unrelated state concerns over the herd's health and residents feeding deer in the region put an end to those trips and forced Matthias to build a new facility behind his resort, where he now keeps a private herd for viewing in a 150-acre preserve.

Next you'll pull up to Elkhorn Cabin overlooking the river, a beautiful rustic red pine building with its fieldstone fireplace glowing. Come on in, dinner's already cookin', presided over by Matthias's wife, Jan. With the help of two antique wood cookstoves, she whips up a gourmet five-course dinner. After enjoying homemade pear and apple crepes, you'll feast on shrimp cocktail, soup, sweet-and-sour salad, crown roast of pork with red-skinned potatoes, and finally white-chocolate-mousse-filled pizzeles with raspberries and white chocolate topping. Then you'll slide back into the sleighs for a starlight-guided ride through the preserve and back to the resort.

On weekends in November, early December, early January, late March, and early April, the elk dinners are punctuated by sleuthing skiers as Thunder Bay Resort offers murder mysteries with dinner.

Norway Ridge Pathway
Mackinaw State Forest, Alpena

Trail type: ▬▬ ⬤

Note: This is a dedicated cross-country and snowshoeing trail area. Snowshoers should stay off the tracks. No dogs are allowed.

Location: About 3.5 miles west of Alpena along Werth Road. From U.S. 23 south of Alpena, head west on Werth and watch for the trailhead parking lot on the right side of the road.

Distance: Three major loops totaling nearly 10 miles round trip. Pathway markers coordinate with maps at the site. Plan on at least three hours to make a round trip.

Terrain: This is a slightly rolling, treed route through a portion of the Mackinaw State Forest. One open section crosses under a power line, which is the only sign of civilization before you return to the parking lot.

Trail difficulty: Easiest to more difficult. Slightly rolling terrain can be handled by all ability levels. No difficult hills.

Surface quality: Double track set. Groomed regularly.

Food and facilities: Food and lodging are available in Hillman to the west (see the separate entry for Thunder Bay Resort) and in Alpena. In Alpena choose from fast-food to sit-down restaurants and accommodations that include the Alpena Holiday Inn, with 148 rooms, an indoor pool, and a whirlpool. Other motels are clustered mostly along MI 32 and U.S. 23. There's a unisex pit toilet at the trailhead, but no water. There's a hospital in Alpena.

Phone numbers: Alpena Convention and Visitors Bureau, (517) 354–4181 or (800) 425–7362. Alpena Holiday Inn, (517) 356–2151. Thunder Bay Resort, (800) 729–9375; Web site, www.thunderbay-golf.com. Local State Department of Natural Resources office, located in Atlanta, (517) 785–4251.

THIS IS ONE of the easier yet more beautiful trails in this region of Michigan. Members of the Youth Conservation Corps cut the trail in the 1970s. Set in a dense old-growth forest scattered with open pockets, it makes for a pleasant trek. There's a choice of four major loops of 1.5, 2.7, about 5, and 5.5 miles. It's relatively flat, so it's a good course for just relaxing and enjoying the scenery; beginners and intermediates can gain confidence. And there's just enough elevation change to give you a good workout. By the time you're back, you'll probably want to change into something dry.

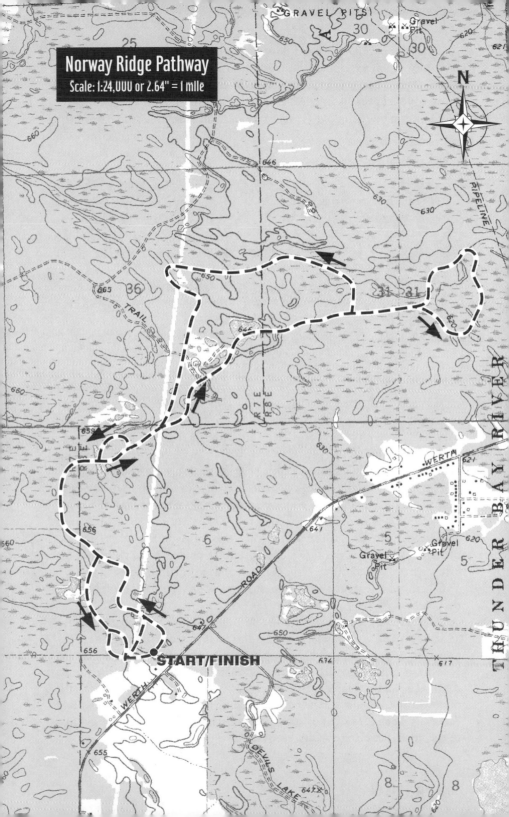

Norway Ridge Pathway
Scale: 1:24,000 or 2.64" = 1 mile

N

GRAVEL PITS

Gravel Pit

30

30

PIPELINE

36

31   31

TRAIL

R 7 E
R 8 E

WERTH

WERTH

Gravel Pit

6

5   5

Gravel Pit

ROAD

START/FINISH

WERTH

DEVILS LAKE

THUNDER BAY RIVER

8   8

From the parking lot head down a short hill; you'll quickly be swallowed by the mostly pine forest. About 0.5 mile into the trail, you'll ski down then cross a power line right-of-way back into the woods. A snow-covered pond is in one clearing just off the trail on your left. From this point on you're in old-growth woods. This is my favorite part of the pathway. Gnarled roots pop up here and there along the trail as you travel up and down slightly rolling humps resulting from trees that fell long ago. Watch for wildlife along the trail, including deer. The largest loop is coming up if you continue past marker 9. It's about 0.75 mile to the next, through stunning old-forest scenery.

Directions at a glance

MILE

0.0   Turn right onto trail from parking lot.

0.2   Pass marker 2.

0.5   Pass marker 6.

1.0   Pass marker 8.

1.2   Turn right at marker 9.

2.2   Turn left at marker 10.

2.6   Turn right at marker 9. Backtrack to start.

Trees are so tall here that they blot out most of the sun and prevent a lot of underbrush from growing, so you can see 100 yards or so through the trees. The trail makes a sweeping left turn right where it intersects with the farthest loop, up and down short, easy hills. Downhill runs are short, but enough to give you a breather. Stop and just enjoy the peace around you. The pathway takes a sharp dogleg left, and you'll nearly double back on the loop before turning right and making a straight run back to marker 9. From this point back to the start you'll be repeating the route you took to get here, including a short uphill jaunt just before the parking lot.

Snowshoers can use the same loops; they're wide enough to accommodate both. Just stay off the tracks. Or—if you've got a compass, for safety's sake—head off to explore the woods in the middle of the loops. You'll eventually meet another one to find your way back by following the markers.

The Alpena area is a gold mine of hiking trails that double in winter as ski routes. They include Thunder Bay Resort near Hillman (see separate entry) and Chippewa Hills, about 12 miles west of U.S. 23 on Nicholson Hill Road. It's another good intermediate series of loops. Along U.S. 23 the Island Park natural area wildlife sanctuary is just north of downtown Alpena and just west of U.S. 23. It's along the Thunder Bay River and open for skiing or snowshoeing. There are more pathways just to the north near Rogers City as well.

Appendix

FOR MORE INFORMATION

Several Michigan organizations stand ready to help skiers find out more information about trails and other facilities available to help them enjoy a Michigan winter. They include:

Michigan Travel Bureau
(888) 78–GREAT
www.michigan.org

Great Lakes Nordic Ski Council
www.skinordic.org
Provides links and a guide to fifteen member-resorts and areas through-out.

West Michigan Tourist Association
(800) 442–2084

Michigan Department of Natural Resources
www.dnr.state.mi.us
Manages all state parks, most of which have cross-country trails.

Huron-Clinton Metroparks
(800) 47–PARKS
www.metroparks.com
These parks ring metro Detroit and offer recreation, including cross-country skiing.

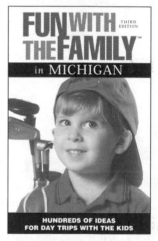

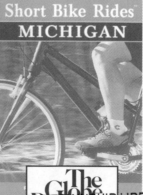